Paul Hamilton Hayne

Avolio - a Legend of the Island of Cos

with Poems, Lyrical, Miscellaneous, and Dramatic

Paul Hamilton Hayne

Avolio - a Legend of the Island of Cos
with Poems, Lyrical, Miscellaneous, and Dramatic

ISBN/EAN: 9783743328693

Manufactured in Europe, USA, Canada, Australia, Japa

Cover: Foto ©ninafisch / pixelio.de

Manufactured and distributed by brebook publishing software (www.brebook.com)

Paul Hamilton Hayne

Avolio - a Legend of the Island of Cos

AVOLIO;

A LEGEND OF THE ISLAND OF COS.

WITH

POEMS,

LYRICAL, MISCELLANEOUS, AND DRAMATIC.

BY

PAUL H. HAYNE.

BOSTON:
TICKNOR AND FIELDS.
M DCCC LX.

Entered according to Act of Congress, in the year 1859, by
TICKNOR AND FIELDS,
in the Clerk's Office of the District Court of the District of Massachusetts.

RIVERSIDE, CAMBRIDGE:
PRINTED BY H. O. HOUGHTON AND COMPANY.

DEDICATORY SONNET

TO EDWIN P. WHIPPLE, ESQ., OF BOSTON.

O FRIEND! between us, for long dreary years,
  Distance and Fate have raised their barriers strong;
  Yet Love, surviving, takes the wings of Song,
  And flies to greet thee; whatsoe'er appears
Of false or feeble in these various lays,
  Forgive; the heart is in them, and to thee
  The lowliest strains of true sincerity
  Rise like the music of a voice of praise.
Though thou hast searched the souls of greatest Seers,
  Shakespeare, and Spencer, Sidney, — to the core
  Of their deep natures probing o'er and o'er, —
Still not the less to humbler bards are given
  Thy faith and homage, — for the Poet's lore,
  Or great or small, is knowledge caught from
    Heaven!

PREFACE.

THE first and longest poem in this volume is founded upon a story contained in that most charming of recent Essayical and Legendary Miscellanies, "The Indicator," by Leigh Hunt. Hunt's story is a version of a very pleasing tradition. Parts of it could in no way be improved. These I have followed literally, but the tale admitted of expansion, and I have, therefore, introduced several new incidents, besides endeavoring to give to the narrative a cast more purely ideal.

The reader will remark that no small portion of this work is composed of Sonnets. Many of these were included in a volume issued from a Southern press in 1857. The edition, originally small, was partially suppressed.

With regard to the Miscellaneous Pieces, I would say, that, excepting five or six poems taken from a collection of more youthful verses, and subjected to the necessary revision, they have before appeared *only* in the columns of literary journals and magazines.

THE AUTHOR.

CONTENTS.

PAGE

Avolio — A Legend of the Island of Cos 1
Ode to Sleep....................................... 17
Ode delivered on the First Anniversary of the Carolina
    Art Association, February 10th, 1859............. 21
Nature the Consoler. An Ode 30

SONNETS.

Poets of the Olden Time............................ 35
On the Occurrence of a Spell of Arctic Weather in
    May, 1858 36
October 37
Great Poets and Small.............................. 38
" Pent in this common Sphere of sensual shows,"..... 39
Ancient Fables..................................... 40
Composed in Autumn 41
" The rainbows of the Heaven are not more rare,".... 42
" Here, friend! upon this lofty ledge sit down!".... 43
" O God! what glorious seasons bless thy world!"... 44
Written on one of the Blue Ridge Range of Mountains 45
" An idle Poet dreaming in the sun,"............... 46
" Yet Stock depreciates, even Banks decay,"......... 47

"Are these the mountains, this the forest gay," 48
"Now, while the Rear-Guard of the flying Year," 49
To W. H. H. 50
Suggested by a Picture of Morning 51

POLITICAL SONNETS.

"Hath the proud Spirit which o'erruled this land," 52
"Strike! 'tis a righteous quarrel! strike as they," 53
"The conflict swells apace! the rallying cries," 54
"Our ancient Honor, our ancestral Pride," 55
"Ay! deaf, blind, lulled with opiates of self-praise," 56
On the refusal of the Legislature of a Southern State to appropriate *any* amount for the Erection of a Monument to the Memory of a distinguished Statesman 57
"Still must the common Voice denounce the deed," 58

MISCELLANEOUS SONNETS.

Suggested by the description of Fairfax Rochester, in chapter xxxvii. of "Jane Eyre" 59
My Study 60
"Belovéd! in this holy hush of night," 61
"O! pour thine inmost soul upon the Air," 62
Shelley 63
Written after reading a description of the burning of Shelley's body 64
Life 65
Death 66
"Thou who art moving ever in the round" 67
"Along the path thy bleeding feet have trod," 68
To W. H. H. 69
"O lady! radiant lady! thy sweet eyes," 70

CONTENTS.

The Mystery of Life	71
The Revelation of Death	72
Preëxistence	73
"Too oft the Poet in elaborate verse,"	74
Elegiac	75
"For aye thou art before me! day and night,"	76
Immaturity	77
"He stands as one to whom all life is vain,"	78
"Between the sunken Sun and the new Moon,"	79
A Character	80
The Garden in the City,	81
"O! weary bondage of the clouding clay,"	82
To a celebrated Actress	83
Written on a fly-leaf of the Letters and Journals of Sir Hudson Lowe, edited by Wm. Forsyth, M. A.	84
After the Storm	85
"Well spake the Poet, that howe'er the cry"	86
Dedicated to M. H. H.	87
The Actor to the Thinker,	88
"All day the distant mountain tops have worn"	89
"The West is one great sea of cloudy fire,"	90

MISCELLANEOUS PIECES.

The Presentiment	91
Queen Galena; or, the Sultana betrayed	93
"The winter Winds may wildly rave,"	95
Lines on the Death of the Rev. J. A. S., the distinguished Pastor of the Church of St. Peter, Charleston, S. C.	96
The Battle in the Distance	99
To a Friend in Affliction	102
The Soul-Conflict	104
Life's under-current	105

CONTENTS.

Song, "Fly, swiftly fly"	107
Song, "Here, long ago,"	109
Song, "Ho! fetch me the winecup! fill up to the brim!"	111
Song of the Naiads	113
Palingenesis	115
The Brook	118
The Poet's Trust in his Sorrow	120
Lines composed upon a beautiful Day in Autumn	122
The Tempter in the House	124
The Unprisoned Spirits	125
The Condemned, a Fragment	127
On a Portrait	128
Sunset and Moonlight	130
The Two Summers	131
The Island in the South	133
The Village Beauty	139
Flowers from a Grave	142
Bought and Sold	143
Perfect Calm	144
Charlotte Brontë	145
Fragment of an Ode on the Death of a great Statesman	147
Lethe	148
January to May	150
A Remembrance	152
The Shadow	154
Lucette	156
The Picture of a beautiful Death, a Fragment	158
Song, "O! your eyes are deep and tender"	161
Lines, "Though dowered with instincts"	162
The Eve of the Bridal	165
"Here, when I have laid aside"	168
My Father	170
The Will, and the Wing,	172

The Pestilence, written during the Prevalence of the Yellow Fever in Charleston, S. C., in the summer of 1858... 174
Retrospection and Aspiration....................... 176
"The laughing Hours before her feet"............... 181
Sonnet. "Vainly a hostile world may strive to tame".. 183
Sonnet, "Moments there are when most familiar things" 184

DRAMATIC SKETCHES.

Antonio Melidori 185
Allan Herbert.................................... 220
Dramatic Fragment 228
Dramatic Fragment................................ 235
The Penitent 236

FUGITIVE VERSES.

"Through dismal nights, and long laborious days"..... 227
A Life-history, — (briefly told).................... 237
To G. C. H....................................... 238
Lines on the Bust of a Bacchante, by Alexander Galt, of Virginia 240
The Realm of Rest................................ 241

POEMS.

AVOLIO — A LEGEND OF THE ISLAND OF COS.

WHAT time the Norman ruled in Sicily
At that mild season when the vernal sea
Is ruffled only by the zephyrs gay,
A goodly ship set sail upon her way
From Ceos unto Smyrna; through the calm
She passed by sunny islands crowned with palm,
Until, so witching tender was the breeze,
So drugged the hours with balms of slumb'rous ease,
That they who manned her, in the genial air
And dalliance of the time, forgot the care
Due to her courses; in the warm sunshine
They lay enchanted, dreaming dreams divine,
Whilst drifting heedless on the halcyon water
The bark obeyed whatever currents caught her.

Borne onward thus for many a charméd day,
They reach at length a wide and wooded bay,
The haunt of birds, whose purpling wings, in flight,

Made even the gold-hued morning seem more bright,
Flushed as with darting rainbows; through the tide
By the o'erripe pomegranate juices dyed,
And laving boughs of the wild fig, and grape,
Great shoals of dazzling fishes madly ape
The play of silver lightnings in the deep
Translucent pools; the crew awoke from sleep,
Or, rather, that strange trance which on them pressed
Gently as sleep; yet still they seemed to rest,
Fanned by voluptuous gales, by Morphean languors
    blessed.

The shore sloped upward into foliaged hills
Cleft by the channels of a maze of rills
That sent their clarion voices clear, and loud,
Up to the answering eagle in the cloud;
Green vales there were between, and pleasant lawns
Thick-set with blooms, like sheen of tropic dawns
Brightening the Orient; further still, the glades
Of murmurous forests flecked with golden shades
Stretched glimmering southward; on the woods' far
    rim,
Faintly discerned through veiling vapors, dim
As mists of Indian summer, the wide view
Was clasped by mountains flickering in the blue
And hazy distance; — over all there hung
The morn's eternal beauty calm and young.

Amidst the throng that gazed with wondering faces
On that fair Eden, and its fairy graces,
Was one — Avolio — a brave youth of Florence,
Self-exiled from his country, in abhorrence
Of the base, blood-stained tyrants dominant there; —
A gentleman he was, of gracious air,
And liberal as the summer, skilled in lore
Of arms, and chivalry, and many more
Deep sciences, which others left unlearned.
He loved adventure; how his spirit burned
Within him, when, as now, a chance arose
To search untravelled forests, and strange foes
Vanquish by púissance of knightly blows,
Or, rescue maidens from malignant spells
Enforced by hordes of wizard sentinels:
So, in the ardor of his martial glee
He clapped his hands, and shouted suddenly:
"Ho! Sirs! a challenge! let us pierce these woods
Down to the core; explore the solitudes,
And make this flowery empire all our own;
Who knows but we may conquer us a throne?
At least, bold feats await us, grand emprise
To win us favor in our ladies' eyes; —
By Heaven! he is a coward who delays!"

So saying, all his countenance ablaze
With fiery zeal, the youth sprang lightly up,

And with right lusty motion filled a cup
(They brought him straightway) to the glistening
    brim
With Cyprus wine: — "Now glory unto him
Whom, bent on gallant deeds, no danger daunts,
Whose constant soul a constant impulse haunts
Which spurs him onward, onward, to the end;
Pledge we the Brave! and may St. Ermo send
Success to crown our valiantest!" this said,
Avolio shoreward leaped, and with him led
The whole ship's company.

               A motley band
Were they who mustered; 'round him on the strand,
Mixed knights, and traders; the first, fired for toil
Which promised glory; the last, hot — for spoil.
Through breezy paths, and beds of blossoming
    thyme
Kept fresh by secret springs, the showery chime
Of whose clear falling waters in the dells,
Played like an airy peal of elfin bells,
With eager minds, but aimless, idle feet,
(The scene about them was so lone, and sweet,
It spelled their steps), 'mid labyrinths of flowers,
By mossy streams, and in deep shadowed bowers,
They strayed from charm to charm through lengths
    of languid hours.

In thickets of wild fern and rustling broom,
The humble-bee buzzed past them with a boom
Of insect thunder, and in glens afar
The golden fire-fly, a small, animate star,
Shone from the twilight of the darkling leaves.
High noon it was, but dusk, like mellow eve's,
Reigned in the wood's deep places, whence it seemed
That flushing locks, and quick arch glances gleamed,
From eyes scarce human; thus the fancy deemed
Of those most given to marvels; the rest laughed
A merry jeering laugh, and many a shaft
Launched from the Norman cross-bow pierced the nooks,
Or cleft the shallow channels of the brooks,
Whence, as the credulous swore, an Oread shy,
And a glad Nymph, had peeped out laughingly.

Thus wandering, they reached a sombre mound
Rising abruptly from the level ground,
And planted thick with dark funereal trees,
Whose foliage waved and murmured, though the breeze
Had sunk to midnight quiet, and the sky
Just o'er the place seemed locked in apathy,
Like a fair face wan with the sudden stroke
Of death, or heart-break; not a word they spoke,

But paused with wide, bewildered, gleaming eyes,
Standing at gaze: what mortal terrors rise
And coil about their hearts with serpent fold;
And O! what loathly scene is this they hold,
Grasped with unwinking vision, as they creep,
(Led by their very horror,) up the steep,
And the whole preternatural landscape dawns
Freezingly on them; a broad stretch of lawns
Sown with rank poisonous grasses, whence the dew
Of hovering exhalations flickered blue,
And wavering on the dead-still atmosphere;
Dead-still it was, and yet the grasses sere,
Stirred as with horrid life amidst the sickening
    glare!

The affrighted crew (all save Avolio) fled
Incontinent, but his dull feet with lead
Seemed freighted; whilst his terror whispered "fly,"
The spell of some uncouth necessity
Baffled retreat, and ruthless, scourged him on;
Meanwhile the sun thro' darkening vapors shone
Nigh to his setting, and a sudden blast —
Sudden and chill — woke shrilly up and passed
With ghostly din, and tumult; airy sounds
Of sylvan horns, and sweep of circling hounds
Nearing the quarry: now, the wizard chase
Swept faintly, faintly up the fields of space,

And now, with backward rushing whirl roared by
Louder, and fiercer, till a maddening cry,
A bitter shriek of human agony
Leaped up, and died, amidst the stifling yell
Of brutes athirst for blood: a crowning swell
Of savage triumph followed, mixed with wails
Sad as the dying songs of nightingales
Murmuring the name — ACTAEON!

    Even as one —
A 'rapt sleep-walker — through the shadows dun
Of half-oblivious sense, with soulless gaze
Goes idly journeying 'midst uncertain ways,
Thus did Avolio, sore perplexed in mind,
(Excess of mystery made his spirit blind,)
Grope through the gloom; anon he reached a fount
Whose watery columns had long ceased to mount
Above its prostrate Tritons: near at hand,
Dammed up in part by heaps of yellow sand, —
Dead-white, and lustreless, — a rivulet
Of oozy banks, with dank dark alders set,
Blurred in its turbid tides the o'erhanging sky;
The melancholy waters seemed to sigh
In wailful murmurs of articulate woe,
And struggling from the sullen depths below,
This dirge arose: —

SONG OF THE IMPRISONED NAIAD.

I.

Woe! woe is me! the ages pass away,
  The mortal seasons run their mystic rounds,
Whilst here I wither for the sun-bright day,
  Its genial sights and sounds.
              Woe! woe is me!

II.

One summer night, in centuries long agone,
  I saw my Oread lover leave the brake,
I heard him plaining on the peaceful lawn
  A plaint "for my sweet sake."
              Woe! woe is me!

III.

Hearkening! I couched upon a reedy bank,
  Until the music grew so mournful-wild,
Its sweet despair o'ercame me, and I sank
  Weak, wailful as a child.
              Woe! woe is me!

IV.

My heart leaped up to answer that fond lay,
  But suddenly the star-girt planets paled,

And high into the welkin's glimmering gray
  Majestic Dian sailed.
                Woe! woe is me!

V.

She swept aloft, — bold, burning as the sun,
  And wrathful-red as fiery-crested Mars;
Then knew I that some fearful deed was done
  On earth, or in the stars,
                Woe! woe is me!

VI.

With ghastly face upraised, and shuddering throat,
  I watched the portent with a prescient pain,
When, lightning-barbed, a beamy arrow smote,
  Or seemed to smite my brain.
                Woe! woe is me!

VII.

Oblivion clasped me, till I woke forlorn,
  Fettered, and sorrowing on this lonely bed,
Shut from the mirthful kisses of the morn, —
  Earth's glories overhead.
                Woe! woe is me!

VIII.

The south winds stir the sedges into song,
  The blossoming myrtles scent the enamored air,

But still, sore moaning for another's wrong,
   I pine in sadness here.
                Woe! woe is me!

IX.

Alas! alas! the weary centuries flee!
   The waning seasons perish, — dark, or bright, —
My grief alone, like some charmed poison-tree,
   Knows not an autumn blight.
                Woe! woe is me!

The mournful sounds swooned off, but Echo rose
And bore them up divinely to a close
Of rare mysterious sweetness; never more
Shall mortal winds to listening wood and shore,
Bring such heart-melting music: "Where, O! where!"
Avolio murmured, "to what haunted sphere
Hath dubious Fate my errant footsteps brought?"
Launched on a baffling sea of mystic thought,
His reason in a whirling chaos lost
Compass and chart, and headway, vaguely tossed
'Midst flitting shapes of wingéd phantasies;—
Just then uplifting his bewildered eyes,
He saw — half hid in shade — the pillars grand,
Of a great gateway reared on either hand,
And close beyond them, nested in a wood
Of stern aspect, a sombrous mansion stood:

Long wreaths of ghastly ivy on its walls
Quivered like goblin tapestry, or palls,
Tattered and rusty, mildewed in the chill
Of dreadful vaults; across each window-sill
Curtains of weird device and fiery hue
Hung moveless,— only when the sun glanced through
The gathering glooms, the hieroglyphs took form,
And life, and action, and the whole grew warm
With meanings baffling to Avolio's sense:—
He stood expectant, trembling, with intense
Dread in his eyes, and yet a struggling faith
Vital at heart;— a sudden-passing breath
Of mystic wind thrilled by his tingling ear,
Waving the curtains inward, and his fear
Uprose victorious, for a serpent shape,
Tall, lithe, and writhing, with malignant gape,
Which showed its fiery fangs, hissed in the gleam
Its own fell eyeballs kindled; oh! supreme
The horror of that vision! as he gazed,
Irresolute, mute, motionless, amazed,
The monster disappeared; a moment sped!
The next, it fawned before him on a bed
Of scarlet poppies. "Speak!" Avolio said,
"What art thou? speak! I charge thee in God's
    name;"

A death-cold shudder seized the Serpent's frame;

Its huge throat writhed; whence, bubbling with a throe
Of hideous import, a voice, thin and low,
Broke like a mudded rill: "Bethink thee well!
This Isle is Cos, of which old legends tell
Such marvels. Hast thou never heard of me, —
The Island's fated Queen?" "Ay! verily!"
Avolio cried, "thou art that thing of dread!" —
Sharply the Serpent raised its glittering head
And front tempestuous. "Hold! no tongue save mine
Shall solve *that* mystery! prithee then, incline
Thine ear to the sad story of my grief,
And with thine ear, yield, yield me thy belief; —
Foul as I am, there *was* a time, O! youth!
When these fierce eyes were founts of love and truth;
There *was* a time when woman's blooming grace
Glowed through the flush of roses in my face;
When, — but I sinned a deep and damning sin, —
I cursed the great Diana! I defied
The night's immaculate goddess, argent-eyed,
And holiest of Immortals! I denied
The eternal might which looks so cold and calm; —
Therefore, O! stranger! am I what I am;
A monster meet for Tartarus! a thing
Whereon men gaze with awe and shuddering,

And stress of inward terror; through all time,
Down to the last age, my abhorrèd crime
Must hold me prisoner in this vile abode,
Unless some man, large-hearted as a god,
Bolder than Ajax, mercifully deign
To kiss me on the mouth!"
                              She towered amain
With sparkling crest, and universal thrill
Of frenzied eagerness that seemed to fill
Her cavernous eyes with jets of lurid fire; —
" And if I do accord thee thy desire,"
Rejoined Avolio, " what sure guage have I,
That this same kiss thy cursèd destiny
Hath not ordained — the least elaborate plan
Whereby to snare and slay me?" " O! man! man!"
The Serpent answered with a loftier mien,
The while her voice grew mild, her front serene,
" Shall *Matter* always triumph; the base mould
Mask the immortal essence, uncontrolled
Save by your grovelling fancies? O! eterne,
And grand Benignities that breathe and burn
Throughout Creation, are we but the motes
In some vain dream that idly sways and floats
To nothingness; or, are your grandeurs pent
Within ourselves, to rise magnificent
In bloom and music, when we bend above,

And wake them by the kisses of our love?
I yearn to be made beautiful; alas!
Beauty itself looks on prepared to pass
In callous disbelief! one action kind,
Would free and save me, — Why art thou so blind
Avolio?" While she spoke, two timorous hares
Scared by a threatening falcon from their lairs,
Rushed to the Serpent's side; with fondling tongue
She soothed them as a mother soothes her young.

Avolio mused. "Can innocent things like these
Take refuge by her? then perchance some good,
Some tenderness, if rightly understood,
Lurks in her nature. *I will do the deed;
Christ and the Virgin save me at my need!*"

He signed the monster nearer, closed his eyes,
And with some natural shuddering, some deep
  sighs,
Gave up his pallid lips to the foul kiss.
What followed then? — a traitorous serpent hiss
Sharper for triumph? O! not so — he felt
A warm, rich, clinging mouth approach and melt
In languid, loving sweetness on his own,
And two fond arms caressingly were thrown
About his neck, and on his bosom pressed
Twin lilies of a pure-white virgin breast.

He raised his eyes, released from brief despair,—
They rested on a maiden tall and fair,
Fair as the tropic morn, when morn is new;
And her sweet glances smote him through and
    through
With such keen-thrilling rapture, that he swore
His willing heart should evermore adore
Such loveliness, and woo her till he died.

"I am thine own," she said, "thine own dear
    bride,
If thou wilt take me." Hand in hand they strayed
Adown the shadows through the woodland glade,
Whence every evil Influence shrank afraid,
And round them poured the golden eventide.

Swiftly the news of this most strange event
Abroad upon the tell-tale wind was sent,
Rousing the eager world to wonderment.

Now 'mid the various companies that came
To visit Cos, was that leal knight by Fame
Exalted, for brave deeds, and faith divine,
Shown in the sacred wars of Palestine,—
Tancred, Salerno's Prince; he came in state,
With fourscore gorgeous barges, small and great;
With pomp and music like an Ocean Fate,

His blazoned prows along the glimmering sea
Spread like an Eastern sunrise gloriously.

Him and his followers did Avolio feast
Right royally, but when the mirth increased,
And joyous-wingéd jests began to pass
Above the sparkling cups of Hippocras,
Tancred arose, and in his courtly phrase
Invoked delight, and length of prosperous days,
To crown that happy union; one sole doubt
The Prince confessed, and this he dared speak out, —
"It could not be that their sweet hostess still
Worshipped Diana, and her heathen will?"
"O! Sir, not so!" Avolio flushing cried,
"But Christ the Lord!" No single word replied
The beauteous lady, but with gentle pride,
And a quick motion to Avolio's side
She drew more closely by a little space,
Gazing with modest passion in his face,
As one who longed to whisper tenderly,
"*O! brave, kind Heart! I worship only thee!*"

ODE TO SLEEP.

I.

Beyond the sunset and the amber sea
To the lone depths of ether, cold, and bare,
Thy influence, Soul of all tranquillity,
Hallows the Earth, and awes the reverent Air;
The gentle Rivulet quells its silvery tune;
The Pines, like priestly watchers, tall and grim,
Stand mute against the saintly Twilight dim,
Breathless to hail the advent of the Moon;
From the white beach the Ocean falls away,
Coyly, and with a thrill; the sea-birds dart
Ghostlike from out the distance, and depart
With a gray fleetness, moaning the dead Day;
The wings of Silence, overfolding Space,
Droop in dusk grandeur from the heavenly steep,
And through the stillness gleams thy starry face,
  Serenest Angel — Sleep.

II.

Come! woo me here, amid these flowery charms;
Breathe on my eyelids; press thy odorous lips
Close to mine own; enwreathe me in thine arms,

And cloud my spirit with thy sweet eclipse.
No dreams, no dreams! keep back the motley throng,
For such are girded round with ghastly might,
And sing low burdens of despondent song,
Decked in the mockery of a lost delight;
I ask Oblivion's balsam — the mute peace,
Toned to still breathings, and the gentlest sighs —
Not music woven of rarest harmonies,
Could yield me such Elysium of release;
The sounds of earth are weariness — not only
'Mid the loud mart, and in the walks of trade,
But where the mountain Genius broodeth lonely,
In the cool pulsing of the sylvan shade;
Then bear me far into thy noiseless land,
Surround me with thy silence, deep on deep,
    Until serene I stand
Close on a duskier country, and more grand,
Mysterious solitude, than thine, O, Sleep!

III.

As he whose veins a feverous frenzy burns,
Whose life-blood withers in the fiery drouth,
Feebly, and with a languid longing turns
To the Spring-breezes gathering from the South,
So feebly, and with languid longing, I
Turn to thy wished nepenthe, and implore
The golden dimness, the purpureal gloom,

Which haunt thy mystic realm, and make the shore
Of thy dominion balmy with all bloom.
In the clear gulfs of thy serene Profound,
Worn Passions sink to quiet, Sorrows pause,
Suddenly fainting to still-breathéd rest;
Thou own'st a magical atmosphere which awes
The memories seething in the turbulent breast,
Which, muffling up the sharpness of all sound
Of mortal lamentation, solely bears
The silvery minor toning of our woe,
And mellowed to harmonious underflow,
Soft as the sad farewells of dying Years,
Lulling as sunset showers that veil the West,
  And sweet as Love's last tears,
When overwelling hearts do mutely weep;
O, Griefs! O, Wailings! your tempestuous madness,
Merged in a regal quietude of sadness,
Wins a strange glory by the streams of Sleep.

IV.

Then woo me here amid these flowery charms;
Breathe on my eyelids; press thy odorous lips
Close to mine own; enfold me in thine arms,
And cloud my spirit with thy sweet eclipse;
And while from waning depth to depth I fall,
Down-lapsing to the utmost depth of all —
Till wan Forgetfulness, obscurely stealing,

Creeps like an Incantation on the soul,
And o'er the slow ebb of my conscious life
Dies the thin flush of the last conscious feeling,
And, like abortive thunder, the dull roll
Of sullen passions swells, — far, far away, —
O, Angel! loose the chords which cling to strife,
Sever the gossamer bondage of my breath —
And let me pass gently, as winds in May,
From the dim realm which owns thy shadowy sway,
To THY diviner sleep, O, sacred Death!

ODE

DELIVERED ON THE FIRST ANNIVERSARY OF THE CAROLINA ART ASSOCIATION, FEBRUARY 10TH, 1859.

I.

There are two worlds wherein our souls may dwell,
Two mighty worlds by eager spirits sought,—
One the loud mart wherein men buy and sell,
The haunt of grovelling Moods, and shapes of Hell,—
The other, that immaculate realm of Thought,
In whose bright Calm the master-workmen wrought,
    Where genius lives on light,
    And faith is lost in sight,
Where the full tides of perfect music swell
Up to the heavens that never held a cloud,
And round great altars reverent hosts are bowed,—
Altars upreared to Love that cannot die,
To beauty that forever keeps its youth,
To kingly Grandeur, and to virginal Truth,
    To all things wise and pure,

Whereof our God hath said, "*endure! endure!*
  Ye are but parts of me,
The HATH BEEN, *and the evermore* TO BE,
Of my supremest Immortality!"

II.

We falter in the darkness and the dearth
Which sordid passions and untamed desires
Create about us; — universal earth
Groans with the burden of our sensual woes;
The heart heaven gave for homage is consumed
By the wild rages of unhallowed fires; —
The blush of that fine glory which illumed
The earlier ages hath gone out in gloom;
There is no joy within us, no repose,
One Creed our beacon, and one God our hold,
  The Creed, the God of Gold;
The heavenward wingèd Instinct that aspires,
Like a lost Seraph with dishevelled plume,
Pants humbled in the "slough of deep Despond;"
The Present binds us, there is no Beyond,
No glorious Future to the soul content
With the poor husks and garbage of this world; —
And are indeed the wings of worship furled
Forevermore? — is no evangel blent,
No sweet evangel — with the hiss and hum
Of th' Century's wheels of progress? SCIENCE
 delves

Down to the Earth's hot vitals, and explores
Realms arctic and antarctic, — the strange shores
Of remote seas, or with raised vision stands,
All undismayed, amidst the starry lands: —
Man too, material man, — our baser selves, —
She hath unmasked even to the source of being;
      Almost she seems a God,
      Deep-searching and far-seeing;
And yet how oft like to a funeral wail
Which goes before the burial of our hopes,
Emerging from the starry-blazoned copes
Of highest firmaments, or darkest vale
O' th' nether earth, or from the burdened air
Of chambers where this mortal frame lies bare,
Probed to the core, — her saddening accents come.
" What! call'st thou man a seraph? nay, a clod,
The veriest clod when this frail breath is spent,
Man shows to us who know him; — what is he?
A speck! the merest dew-globe 'midst the sea
      Of Life's infinity;" —
Or, "we have probed, dissected all we can, —
But never yet, in any mortal man,
Found we the spirit! thing of time and clay,
Eat, drink, live well thy transient insect-day!"
Thus SCIENCE; but whilst still her mocking voice
Rings with a cold sharp clearness in our ears,
Her beauteous sister, on whose brow the years

Have left no cankering vestige of decay,—
Eternal ART,—she of the fathomless eyes
Brimming with light, half worship, half surprise,
In whose right hand a branch of fadeless palms,
Plucked from the depths of golden-shadowed calms,
      Points upward to the skies,—
She answers in a minor, sweet and strange,
[The while, all graces in her aspect meet,
And Doubt and Fear shrink shuddering at her feet,]
"I bring a nobler message! Soul, rejoice!
Rise with me from thy troublous toils of sense,
Thy bootless struggles, born of impotence,
Rise to a subtler view, a broader range
      Of thought and aim;—
      Mine is a sway ideal,
But still the works I prompt, alone, are real;
Mine is a realm from immemorial time
Begirt by Deeds and Purposes sublime,
Whose consecration is Faith's quenchless flame,
Whose voices are the songs of poet-sages,
Whose strong foundations resting on the ages,
The throes and crash of Empires have not shaken,—
Nor any futile force of human rages.

      Come! let us enter in!
Behold, the portal gates stand open wide!
Only, from off thy spirit shake the dust

Of any thought of sin,
Or sordid pride,
For sacred is the kingdom of my trust,
By Mind, and Strength, and Beauty sanctified.

She spoke! and o'er the threshold of a sphere,
A marvellous sphere, they passed;
From the deep bosom of the purpling air
A lambent glory broke along the vast
Horizon line, whence clouds, like incense, rolled
Athwart a firmamental arc of gold
And sapphire, — clouds not vapour-born,
But clasping each the radiant seeds of morn,
Which sudden, the clear zenith heights attained,
Burst into light, unfolding like a flower,
From out whose quivering heart a mystic shower
Of splendor rained:
A spell was Her's to conquer time and space,
For from the desert grandeur of that place
A hundred temples rise,
The marble poems of the Bards of old,
Whereon, 'twere well to look with reverent eyes,
Because they body noblest Aspirations,
Ethereal Hopes, and winged Imaginations, —
Whether to fabled Jove their walls were raised,
Or on their inner altars offerings blazed
To wise Athéna, or, in Christian Rome

Beneath St. Peter's mighty circling dome,
— A second Heaven — the golden censers swing,
The clear-toned choirs those hymns of rapture sing,
Which, on harmonious waves of gratulation,
The outburst of the sense of deep salvation,
Uplift the spirit where the INCARNATE WORD
Amidst the praise no ear of man hath heard,
The peace no mind of man can comprehend,
Awaits to welcome Time's poor wanderers home!

"But look again!" Art's eager Genius cried,
  "Thou hast not seen the end,
Scarce the beginning!" — as she spake, a tide
Of all the mighty Masters, loved, adored,
From out the shining distant spaces poured, —
All those who fashioned — through an inward dower —
The concrete forms of Beauty and of Power;
Whether from white Pentelic quarries brought;
The voiceless stone uprose — a breathing Thought,
Or, from the gorgeous rays of rainbows drawn,
And colors of the sunset and the dawn,
The PAINTER's pencil his ideal fine,
  Had clothed in hues divine —
  Or, skilled in living words
Melodious as the natural voice of birds,
But each a sentient thing, a meaning grand,
It is not given to all to understand,

The Poet from the shade of breezy woods,
    From barren seaside solitudes,
And from the pregnant quiet of his soul
Outbreathed the numbers that forever roll,
Perennial as the fountains of the sea,
And deep almost as deep Eternity!

Near and yet nearer the bright concourse came,
    Their faces all a-flame,
As when of yore the quick creative thrill
Did smite them into utterance, and the throng,
Awed by the fiery burden of the song,
    Grew reverent pale and still;
O! solemn and sublime Apocalypse
That wresteth, from the dreary death-eclipse,
The sacred presence of these wondrous men!
Yonder the visible Homer moves again,
    Moves as he moved below,
    Save that his smitten vision,
Rekindled at a fount of fire Elysian,
Burns with a subtler, grander, deeper glow:
And yonder Æschylus, with "thunderous brow,"
Scarred by the lightning of his own creations,
Wrapped in a cloud of sombre meditations,
Hath seized the Tragic Muse, as if to her
He scorned to bend an humble worshipper,
    But would extort her gifts;

Then Shakspeare mild,
Blessed with the innocent credence of a child,
With a child's thoughts, and fancies undefiled, —
    And yet — a Magian strong,
To whom the springs of terrible fears belong,
Of majesty, and beauty, and delight;
To the wierd charm of whose infallible sight,
    The heart's emotions,
Though turbid as the tides of darkest oceans,
Shone clear as water of the woodland brooks, —
Passed with high wisdom thronéd in his looks
Attempered by the genial heats of wit;
Whilst close beside him — his grand countenance lit
By thoughts like those which wrought his Judgment
  Day,
    Grave Michel Angelo
    His massive forehead lifts,
In a strange Titan fashion, unto Heaven; —
Next Raphael comes with calm and star-like mien,
Fresh from the Beatific Ecstacy,
His face how beautiful, and how serene!
Since God for him the awful veil had riven,
    That shrouds Divinity, —
And rolled before his wondering mind and eye
Visions that WE should gaze on but — to die!

They passed, and thousands more passed by with
  them;

Again Art's Genius spake: "Lo! these are they
      Who, through stern tribulations,
Have raised to Right and Truth the subject nations;
      Lo! these are they,
Who, were the whole bright concourse swept away,
Their fame's last barrier built the surge to stem
Of chaos and oblivion, whelmed beneath
The pitiless torrent of eternal death,
Would yet bequeath to races unbegot,
The precepts of a faith which faileth not;
Pointing, from troublous toils of time and sense,
From bootless struggles born of impotence,
      To that fair Realm of Thought,
In whose bright Calm these master-workmen wrought,
Where the full tides of perfect music swell
Up to the heavens that never held a cloud,
And round great Altars worshipping hosts are bowed, —
Altars upreared to Love that cannot die,
To Beauty that forever keeps its youth,
To kingly Grandeur, and to virginal Truth,
      To all things wise and pure,
Whereof our God hath said, — "*Endure, endure!*
      Ye are but parts of me,
The Hath Been, *and the evermore* To Be
Of my supremest Immortality!"

NATURE THE CONSOLER.

AN ODE.

I.

Gladly I hail these Solitudes, and breathe
The inspiring breath of the fresh woodland air,
Most gladly to the Past alone bequeathe
    Doubt, Grief, and Care;
I feel a new-born freedom of the mind,
Nursed at the breast of Nature, with the dew
Of glorious dawns; I hear the mountain wind,
— Clear as if Elfin trumpets loudly blew, —
Peal through the dells, and scale the lonely height,
Rousing the echoes to a quick delight,
Bending the forest monarchs to its will,
'Till all their ponderous branches shake and thrill
In the wide-wakening tumult; far above
The Heavens stretch calm and blessing; far below
The mellowing fields are touched with evening's
    glow,
And many pleasant sights and sounds I love,
Would gently woo me from all thoughts of woe:
Sunlighted meadows, — music in the grove,

From happy bird-throats, and the fairy rills
That lapse in silvery murmurs through the hills;
Great circles of rich foliage, rainbow-crowned
By Autumn's liberal largess,— whilst around
Grave sheep lie musing on the pastoral ground,
    Or, sending a mild bleat
    To other flocks afar,
The fleecy comrades they are wont to meet,
Homeward returning 'neath the vesper star!

II.

O! genial peace of Nature! divine calm
That fallest on the spirit, like the rain
Of Eden, bearing melody and balm
To soothe the troubled heart and heal its pain,
Thy influence lifts me to a realm of joy,
A moonlight happiness, intense but mild,
Unvisited by shadow of alloy,
And flushed with tender dreams and fancies undefiled.

III.

The universe of God is still, not dumb,
For many voices in sweet undertone
    To reverent listeners come,—
And many thoughts, with truth's own honey laden
Into the watcher's wakeful brain have flown,

Charming the inner ear
With harmonies so low, and yet so clear,
So undefined, yet pregnant with a feeling,
An inspiration of sublime revealing, —
That they whose being the strong spell shall hold,
    Do look on earthly things,
Through atmospheres of rich imaginings,
    And find in all they see,
    A meaning manifold;
The forces of divine vitality
Break through the sensual gloom
    About them furled,
All instinct with the radiant grace and bloom
Caught from the glories of a lovelier world.

IV.

A lovelier world! in the thronged space on high,
Dwells there indeed a fairer Star than ours,
Circled by sunsets of more gorgeous dye,
And gifted with an ampler wealth of flowers?
Can heavenly bounty lavish richer stores
Of color, fragrance, beauty and delight
    On mortal, or immortal sight,
In any sphere that rolls around the sun?
See what a splendor from the dying day
Through the grand forest pours!
Now, lighting up its veteran-crests with glory,

Now slanting down the shadows dim and hoary,
Till, in the long-drawn gloom of leafy glades,
At the far close of their impervious shades,
The purple splendor softly melts away!

v.

Now, overarched by dewy canopies,
And awed by dimness that is hardly gloom,
We stand amidst the silence with hushed lips,
Watching the dubious glimmer of the skies
Paled by the foliage to a half-eclipse,
  And struggling for full room,
With intermittent gleams, that quickly die
In throbs and tremors, waning suddenly
To the mere ghosts of flame, to Apparitions
Impalpable as star-beams in deep seas,
Lost in the dark below the surface-ruffling breeze.

vi.

Latest of all these marvellous transitions,
And crowning all with unsurpasséd grace,
The eyes of the night's Empress, witching-sweet,
Scatter the shadows in each secret place,
So that where'er her beamy glances fleet,
Shot through and through, as if with arrowy might,
The dusky Gloaming falls before her shafts of light.

VII.

Soothed by this milder glory, let us pass
To the weird land of peace-embosomed dreams,
The lapsing of the far-off forest streams
    Rustling the reedy grass,
Will make rare music for us, till we reach
    The mystic beach,
The margin of the starry sea of sleep;
Thence, launching on the waters, let us sail
Beneath a Heaven of ever-living blue,
Thronged with fair loving faces, fair though pale,
The faces of the faithful souls we knew
In our glad youth, before the death-clouds lowered; —
O! let us hold them in communion deep,
And learn, although our lower world is fair,
    A lovelier sphere,
Circled by sunlights of more gorgeous dye,
And gifted with an ampler wealth of flowers,
Dwells in the unimagined heights of Air,
Unmeasured by dull Time, the weary-houred, —
And further learn, *that* world shall yet be ours,
Wherein, released from every human care,
The Mortal puts on Immortality!

SONNETS.

POETS OF THE OLDEN TIME.

The brave old Poets sing of nobler themes
Than the weak griefs which haunt men's coward
    souls;
The torrent of their lusty music rolls
Not through dark valleys of distempered dreams,
But murmurous pastures lit by sunny streams;
Or, rushing from some mountain height of Thought,
Swells to strange meaning that our minds have
    sought
Vainly to gather from the doubtful gleams
Of our more gross perceptions. O, their strains
Nerve and ennoble manhood!—no shrill cry,
Set to a treble, tells of querulous woe;
Yet numbers deep-voiced as the mighty Main's
Merge in the ringdove's plaining, or the sigh
Of lovers whispering where sweet streamlets flow.

SONNET.

ON THE OCCURRENCE OF A SPELL OF ARCTIC WEATHER IN MAY, 1858.

WE thought that Winter with his hungry pack
Of hounding Winds had closed his dreary chase,—
For virgin Spring, with arch, triumphant face,
Lightly descending, had strewed o'er his track
Gay flowers that hid the stormy season's wrack.
Vain thought! for, wheeling on his northward path,
And girt by all his hungry Blasts, in wrath
The shrill-voiced Huntsman hurries swiftly back,—
The frightened vernal Zephyrs shrink and die
Through the chilled forest,— the rare blooms expire,—
And Spring herself, too terror-struck to fly,
Seized by the ravening Winds with fury dire,
Dies 'mid the scarlet flowers that round her lie,
Like waning flames of some rich funeral fire!

OCTOBER.

The passionate Summer's dead! — the sky's aglow
With roseate flushes of matured desire,
The winds at eve are musical and low
As sweeping chords of a lamenting lyre,
Far up among the pillared clouds of fire,
Whose pomp in grand procession upward grows
With gorgeous blazonry of funeral shows
To celebrate the Summer's past renown;
Ah me! How regally the Heavens look down
O'ershadowing beautiful autumnal woods,
And harvest-fields with hoarded increase brown,
And deep-toned majesty of golden floods,
That lift their solemn dirges to the sky,
To swell the purple pomp that floateth by.

GREAT POETS AND SMALL.

Shall I not falter on melodious wing,
In that my notes are weak and may not rise
To those world-wide entrancing harmonies,
Which the great Poets to the ages sing?
Shall my thought's humble heaven no longer ring
With pleasant lays, because the Empyreal height
Doth stretch beyond it, lifting to the light
The Titan pinion of song's sun-crowned King?
'Tis a false thought! the thrush a fitful flight
Ventures in vernal dawns; a happy note
Trills from the russet linnet's gentle throat,
Though far above the eagle soars in might,
And the glad skylark — an etherial mote —
Sings in high realms that mock our straining sight.

SONNET.

Pent in this common Sphere of sensual shows,
I pine for beauty; beauty of fresh mien,
And gentle utterance, and the charm serene,
Wherewith the hue of mystic dream-land glows;
I pine for lulling music, the repose
Of low-voiced waters, in some realm between
The perfect Aidenn, and this clouded scene
Of love's sad loss, and passion's mournful throes;
A pleasant country, girt with twilight calm,
In whose fair heaven a moon of shadowy round
Wades through a fading fall of sunset rain;
Where drooping lotos-flowers, distilling balm,
Gleam by the drowsy streamlets Sleep hath crown'd,
And Care forgets to sigh, and Patience conquers
    Pain.

ANCIENT FABLES.

Ye pleasant myths of Eld, why have ye fled?
The earth has fallen from her blissful prime
Of summer years, — the dews of that sweet time
Are withered on its garlands sere and dead.
No longer in the blue fields overhead
We list the rustling of immortal wings,
Or hail at eve the kindly visitings
Of gentle Genii to fair fortunes wed:
The seas have lost their Nereids, the sad streams
Their gold-haired habitants, — the mountains lone
Those happy Oreads, and the blithsome tone
Of Pan's soft pipe melts only in our dreams;
Fitfully fall the old Faith's broken gleams
On our dull hearts, cold as sepulchral stone.

SONNET.

COMPOSED IN AUTUMN.

WITH these dead leaves stripped from a withered tree,
And slowly fluttering round us, gentle Friend,
Some faithless soul a sad presage might blend; —
To me they bring a happier augury; —
Lives that shall bloom in genial sunshine free,
Nursed by the spell Love's dews and breezes send,
And when a kindly Fate shall speak the end,
Down dropping in Time's autumn silently;
All hopes fulfilled, all passions duly blessed,
Life's cup of gladness drained — except the lees,
No more to fear or long for, but the rest
Which crowns existence with its dreamless ease:
Thus when our days are ripe, oh! let us fall
Into that perfect Peace which waits for all!

SONNET.

The rainbows of the Heaven are not more rare,
More various and more beautiful to view,
Than these rich forest rainbows, dipped in dew
Of morn and evening, glimmering on the air
From wooded dell and mountain-summit fair;
O! Autumn! wonderous Painter! every hue
Of thy immortal pencil is steeped through
With essence of divinity; how bare
Beside thy coloring the poor shows of Art,
Though Art were thrice inspired; in dreams alone
(The loftiest dreams wherein the soul takes part)
Of jasper pavements, and the sapphire Throne
Of Heaven, hath such unearthly brightness shone
To flush, and thrill the visionary heart!

SONNET.

Here, friend! upon this lofty ledge sit down!
And view the beauteous prospect spread below,
Around, above us; in the noon-day glow
How calm the landscape rests!—'yon distant town,
Enwreathed with clouds of foliage like a crown
Of rustic honor; the soft, silvery flow
Of the clear stream beyond it, and the show
Of endless wooded heights, circling the brown
Autumnal fields, alive with billowy grain;
Say! hast thou ever gazed on aught more fair
In Europe, or the Orient?—what domain
(From India to the sunny slopes of Spain)
Hath beauty, wed to grandeur in the air,
Blessed with an ampler charm, a more benignant
    reign?

SONNET.

O God! what glorious seasons bless thy world!
See! the tranced winds are nestling on the deep;
The guardian Heavens unclouded vigil keep
O'er the mute Earth; the beach birds' wings are
    furled,
Ghost-like and gray, where the dim billows, curled
Lazily up the sea-strand, sink in sleep,
Save when a random fish with lightning leap
Flashes above them; the far sky's impearled
Inland, with lines of silvery smoke that gleam
Upward from quiet homesteads, thin, and slow;
The sunset girds me like a gorgeous dream,
Pregnant with splendors, by whose mystical spell
Senses and soul are flushed to one deep glow,
A purple-vestured Mood, more grand than words
    may tell.

SONNET.

WRITTEN ON ONE OF THE BLUE RIDGE RANGE OF MOUNTAINS.

Here let me pause by the lone eagle's nest,
And breathe the golden sunlight and sweet air,
Which gird and gladden all this region fair,
With a perpetual benison of rest;
Like a grand Purpose that some god hath blest,
The immemorial mountain seems to rise,
Yearning to overtop diviner skies,
Though monarch of the pomps of East and West;
And pondering here, the Genius of the height,
Quickens my soul as if an angel spake,
And I can feel old chains of custom break,
And old Ambitions start to win the light;
A calm resolve born with them, in whose might
I thank thee, Heaven! that noble thoughts awake.

SONNET.

I.

An idle Poet dreaming in the sun, —
One given to much unhallowed vagrancy
Of thought and step; who, when he comes to die,
In the broad world can point to nothing done;
No chartered corporations, no streets paved
With very princely stone-work, no vast file
Of warehouses, no slowly-hoarded pile
Of priceless treasure, no proud sceptre waved
O'er potent realms of stock, no magic art
Lavished on curious gins, or works of steam;
Only — a few wild songs that melt the heart;
Only — the glow of some unearthly dream,
Embodied and immortal! What are these,
Sneers the sage world, — chaff! smoke! vain
    phantasies!

SONNET.

II.

Yet Stock depreciates, even Banks decay,
Merchant and architect are lowly laid
In purple palls, and the shrewd lords of trade
Lament, for they *were* wiser in their day
Than the clear sons of light; — but prithee, how
Doth stand the matter, when the years have fled;
What means yon concourse thronging where the dead
Old Singer sleeps; — say! do they seek him *now?*
Now that his dust is scattered on the breath
Of every wind that blows; — what meaneth this?
It means, thou sapient citizen, that death
Heralds the Bard's true life, as with a kiss,
Wakens *two immortalities;* then bow
To the world's scorn, O Poet, with calm brow.

SONNET.

ARE these the mountains, this the forest gay,
Through whose grand gorges, and empurpled aisles
I walked when Nature wore the light of smiles,
And tuneful Fancies charmed the genial way?
O'er the broad landscape shines as fair a day,
Still sport the breezes, and the wild brooks weave
The same low, drowsy, music; wherefore grieve,
I ask my heart, and whence this sad decay
Of answering gratulation? Oh! my soul,
In thee, in thee, the mournful darkness lies,
Which clogs the buoyant pulse, and dims the eyes
That feasted once upon the humblest flowers;
And so, in vain the kingly mountain towers,
The joyous forest waves, the sparkling waters roll.

SONNET.

Now, while the Rear-Guard of the flying Year,
Rugged December, on the season's verge
Marshals his pale Days to the mournful dirge
Of muffled winds in far-off forests drear,
Good friend! turn with me to our in-door cheer;
Draw nigh, the huge flames roar upon the hearth,
And this sly sparkler is of subtlest birth,
And a rich vintage, poet souls hold dear;
Mark how the sweet rogue woos us! Sit thee down,
And we will quaff, and quaff, and drink our fill,
Topping the spirits with a Bacchanal crown,
Till the funereal blast shall wail on more,
But silver-throated clarions seem to thrill,
And shouts of triumph peal along the shore.

SONNET.

TO W. H. H.

I PRAY the Angel in whose hands the sum
Of mortal fates in mystic darkness lies,
That to the soul which fills these deepening eyes,
Sun-crowned and clear, the SPIRIT OF SONG may
    come;
That strong-winged Fancies, with melodious hum
Of pluméd vans, may touch to sweet surprise
His poet nature, born to glow and rise,
And thrill to worship though the world be dumb;
That Love, and Will, and Genius, all may blend
To make HIS soul a guiding star of Time,
True to the purest thought, the noblest end,
Full of all richness, gentle, wise, complete,
In whose still heights, and most ethereal clime,
Beauty, and Faith, and plastic Passion meet.

SONNET.

SUGGESTED BY A PICTURE OF MORNING.

The darkness pales in Heaven; the eyes of Morn
Unclose from out the Orient; purple bars
Of tender sunlight dim the o'erwearied stars,
And the wan moon withdraws her watery horn,
Lost in the Dayspring's rising; Life is born
From the glad heart of Nature, roused anew
To pulse in freedom through the deepening blue
Of tranquil skies, to bend the golden corn
In broad savannahs, and to stir the sea
With odorous breezes rippling into calm,
Where by the still lagoons, the pensive palm
Doth take the winds' faint kisses languidly;
While the earth's various voices blend in one
Harmonious *Jubilate* to the Sun.

POLITICAL SONNETS.

SONNET.

I.

HATH the proud Spirit which o'erruled this land
When Freedom was baptized in holy blood,
Succumbed forever to the turbid flood
Of wretched anarchies!—oh! calm and grand,
Did her broad wings above our homes expand
In the old heroic days; but we have turned
From the high shrine whereon her glories burned,
And her sweet tongue none seem to understand.
What! battling by our hearthstones, while the Foe
Storms at the gates of our most sacred Right,
When every limb should girded be for fight,
And every heart with one impulsion glow!
Let Traitors in base broils expend their might,
A Titan threats us — shall we bide the blow?

II.

STRIKE! 'tis a righteous quarrel! strike as they,
Our grand, brave, free Ancestors struck of yore,
Full at the Tyrant's bosom — they forebore,
But not so long as we have — much delay
Endangers liberty, and Freedom's day
Wanes when the unquelled Despot stalks abroad.
Why pause ye? right is right, and God is God
Forever — while the mountain breezes play
Unfettered round your summits, while the sea
Breaks on your shores in thunder, and the glooms
Of mighty woods enshroud your Patriots' tombs,
Ringing to stormy anthems, can it be
That ye will court the Oppressor's insolent sway,
And basely fawn, and falter, and — obey?

SONNET.

I.

The conflict swells apace! the rallying cries
Of frenzied Faction, and discordant Hate
Send forth their ominous voices, thundering fate
And ruin, while all loftier virtue dies!
Above us gleam two giant Destinies
Solemn and still, the one with mien elate,
The other that dread Doom whose shadows wait
Where Freedom's sun pales down its wintry skies;
Behind us looms the Past, innumerous grand
Imperial Phantoms resurrectionized,
And beckoning with dumb pathos by their tombs,—
Beyond us, the veiled Future, with command
To bless or curse, as we shall stand full-sized
In Freedom's light, or dwarfed in Slavery's glooms.

II.

Our ancient Honor, our ancestral Pride,
Duty, and manhood, every regal Thought
Wherewith a noble end is nobly wrought,
Purpose made strong and Valor sanctified,
All urge divorce from that weak sloth allied
To treacherous peace by glozing compacts bought;
Success, and empire shall not come unsought,
And pluméd Victory walks by Labor's side;
Yet Sleep hath bound us, and the shadow of dreams
Rests cold upon our spirits; one by one
The bulwarks of supremest Rights are riven,
And the crash wakes us not, the lightning-gleams
Unheeded o'er the tempest's bosom run,
And we are blind and deaf to earth, and — heaven.

III.

Ay! deaf, blind! lulled with opiates of self-praise,
And sluggish in the calm of base content;
Our Wisdom clogged, our Will in banishment,
Idly we pass the weak, voluptuous days;
Or, if a moment starting from the maze
Of pleasant dreamings, we have feebly bent
To mark the insurgent Madness which hath rent
The altars of our safety, brief the gaze!
Straight the lethargic Ease resumes its power,
And with a listless, and all-vacant air,
We mutter foolish fancies, and — are still;
Meantime, the Foe is up, the trumpets blare,
The mailed Oppression works his iron will,
Whilst dark Destruction bides the final Hour.

SONNET.

I.

[On the refusal of the Legislature of a Southern State to appropriate *any* amount for the erection of a Monument to the memory of a distinguished Statesman.]

YE cannot add by any pile YE raise
One jot, or tittle to the Statesman's fame:
That the world knows; to the far future days
Belongs his glory, and its radiant flame
Will burn when YE are dead, decayed, forgot;
Therefore your opposition matters not;
The thin-masked jealousies of present time
Unburied in his grave, survive to keep
Rampant the hate HE deemed his highest praise,
And the rude clash of discord o'er his sleep;
But for his great, wise acts, his faith sublime,
ALL that the soul of genius sanctifies,
These mount where viler Passions cannot climb,
These live where palsied Malice faints and dies.

II.

Still must the common Voice denounce the deed,
The common Heart swell with an outraged pride,
That the poor purchase of the paltry meed
His country owed him, should be thus denied;
Shame on the Senate! shame on every hand
Which did not falter when recording there,
The basest act achieved for many a year,
To fire the scorn of the whole Southern land;
Nor the South only, for our foes will cry,
Out on your petty pasteboard chivalry!
The People who refuse to crown the Great
And Good with honor, do themselves eclipse,
And doubly shameless is the recreant State,
Whose condemnation comes from her own lips.

SONNET.

SUGGESTED BY THE DESCRIPTION OF FAIRFAX ROCHESTER, IN CHAP. XXXVII. OF "JANE EYRE."

He stands beneath the bleak, bare Heavens alone,
The baffled passions smouldering in his face,
Hopeless of mercy and apart from grace,
And rigid as some monument of stone;
All but his innate manhood overthrown,
That iron Hardihood which turns on Fate,
Uplifts the Despot's gauntlet — fronts his hate,
With fiery eyes unquailing as his own;
Within, the maddening sorrows chafe and swell,
The pent volcano stirs its depths of fire,
But the firm lips are voiceless, and the knell
Of love, and hope, and the consuming ire
Of thwarted longing, find nor word nor groan.
O Man! that stand'st beneath the Heavens alone!

MY STUDY.

This is my world! within these narrow walls,
I own a princely service; the hot care
And tumult of our frenzied life are here,
But as a ghost, and echo; what befalls
In the far mart to me is less than nought;
I walk the fields of quiet Arcadies,
And wander by the brink of hoary seas,
Calmed to the tendance of untroubled Thought:
Or if a livelier humor should enhance
The slow-timed pulse, 'tis not for present strife,
The sordid zeal with which our Age is rife,
Its Mammon conflicts crowned by Fraud or Chance,—
But gleamings of the lost, heroic life,
Flushed through the gorgeous vistas of Romance.

SONNET.

I.

BELOVÉD! in this holy hush of night,
I know that thou art looking to the South, —
Fair face, and fair white forehead bathed in the
    light
Of tender Heavens, and o'er thy delicate mouth
A dewy gladness from thy dark eyes shed;
O! eloquent eyes, that on the evening spread
The glory of a radiant world of dreams,
(The inner moonlight of the heart that dims
This moonlight of the sense), and o'er thy head
Thrown back as listening to a voice of hymns
Perchance in thine own spirit, violet-gleams
From modest flowers that deck the window bars,
While the winds sigh, and sing the far-off streams,
And a faint bliss seems dropping from the stars.

II.

O! POUR thine inmost soul upon the Air,
And trust to Heaven the secrets that recline
In the sweet nunnery of thy virgin breast;
Speak to the winds that wander everywhere, —
And sure must wander hither — the divine
Contentment, and the infinite, deep rest
That calm thy passionate being, and lift high
To the still realm of Love's eternity
The passive ocean of thy charméd thought;
And tell the Ariel element to bear
The burden of thy whispered heart to me,
By Fairy alchemy of distance wrought
To something sacred as a saintly prayer,
A spell to set my nobler nature free.

SHELLEY.

BECAUSE they thought his doctrines were not just
Mankind assumed for him the chastening rod,
And Tyrants reared in pride, and strong in lust,
Wounded the noblest of the sons of God;
The heart's most cherished benefactions riven,
They strove to humble, blacken, and malign
A soul whose charities were wide as Heaven,
Whose *deeds*, if not his *doctrines*, were divine;
And in the name of HIM whose sunshine warms
The evil as the righteous, deemed it good
To wreak their bigotry's relentless storms
On one whose nature was not understood;
Ah well! God's ways are wonderous — it *may* be
His seal hath not been set to man's decree.

SONNET.

WRITTEN AFTER READING TRELAWNEY'S DESCRIPTION OF THE BURNING OF SHELLEY'S BODY.

Why did they take thee from thine Ocean-grave,
O! man of many sorrows?—the blue sea
Had been thy brother, and each wandering wave
That kissed the shores of thy loved Italy
A solace, and a blessing:—the low moan
Of the lamenting waters seemed to start
Within thy soul an echo, and the tone
Of a more mournful music in thy heart.
O! therefore did'st thou seek them, and pour forth
To their deep sympathy a sorrowing strain
Of all the woes and wretchedness of earth,
That strove to bend thy patient mind in vain:
The Ocean heard thee, loved thee—and the breast
Of Nature's mighty minstrel gave thee—rest.

LIFE.

I.

Suffering! — and yet magnificent in pain!
Mysterious! — yet like spring-showers in the sun
Veiling the light with their melodious rain,
Life from the worlds beyond hath radiance won;
Its gloomiest phase is as the clouds that mourn
'Neath the majestic brightness of the Arch,
Where nobler orbs in deathless daylight burn,
And God's great pulses beat their music-march:
The Heaven we worship dimly, girt with tears,
The spirit Heaven! what is it but a Life,
Lifting its soul beyond our mortal years
That oft begin, and ever end in strife;
Strife we must pass to win a happier Height;
Nature but travails to reveal us — light.

DEATH.

II.

THEN whence, O Death, thy dreariness? We know
That every flower the breeze's flattering breath
Woos to a blush, and love-like murmuring low,
Dies but to multiply its bloom in death;
The rill's glad prattling infancy, that fills
The woodlands with its song of innocent glee,
Is passing through the heart of shadowy hills
To swell the eternal Manhood of the Sea;
And the great Stars, Creation's minstrel-fires,
Are rolling toward the central source of Light,
Where all their separate glory but expires,
To merge into ONE WORLD'S unbroken might;
There is no death but change, soul claspeth soul,
And all are portion of the Immortal whole.

SONNET.

Thou who art moving ever in the round
Of Custom, dragging an eternal chain,
Whose weight for thy dull spirit hath no pain,
Deeming that thou life's secret bliss hast found;—
Whose senseless ear is ravished by no sound
Of inner harmonies, whose eyes are blind
To the rich splendors of creative mind,
That make our common earth imperial ground,
'Tis well for thee in the supreme content
Of grovelling worldliness, to sit, and sigh
That Heaven hath fashioned Poesy, and blent
With our base instincts aught of pure, and high;
Thou would'st pluck down the stars, and curb the bound
Of Ocean, did thy Avarice gain thereby!

SONNET.

Along the path thy bleeding feet have trod,
O Christian Mother! do the martyr-years,
Crownéd with suffering, through the mist of tears
Uplift their brows — thorn-circled — unto God;
Most bitterly our Father's chastening rod
Hath ruled within thy term of mortal days,
Yet in thy soul spring up the tones of praise,
Freely as flowers from out a burial-sod:
Nor hath a tireless Faith essayed in vain
To win from sorrow that diviner rest,
Which, like a sunset, purpling through the rain
Of dying storms, maketh the darkness blest;
Grief is transfigured, and dethronéd Fears
Pale in the glory beckoning from the West.

SONNET.

TO W. H. H.

How like a mighty picture, tint by tint,
This marvellous world is opening to thy view!
Wonders of earth and heaven; shapes bright and new,—
Strength, radiance, beauty, and all things that hint
Most of the primal glory, and the print
Of Angel footsteps;— from the globe of dew
Tiny, but luminous, up to the circling Blue
Unbounded — thou drink'st knowledge without stint;
Like a pure blossom nursed by genial Winds,
Thy innocent life, expanding day by day,
Upsprings, spontaneous, to the perfect flower;
Lost Eden-splendors round thy pathway play,
And o'er it rise and burn the starry Signs
Which herald hope, and joy, to souls of power.

SONNET.

O LADY! radiant lady! thy sweet eyes,
And happy smiles, and fulness of all light
Of genial beauty, overthrong my sight
With memories of another, who now lies
Crowned with the churchyard marble: thou hast all
Her winning graces, and her blighted years
Re-bloom in thee, — the dark thought disappears
That wooed the silence, and o'erwept the pall.
My soul flows to thee, and though not again
May passionate thoughts possess me, I will pray,
(As a fond brother might,) that on thy way
The adoration of strong love may rain
Its benedictions, — and around thee fall
Blisses that deepen with the deepening day.

THE MYSTERY OF LIFE.

I.

Wrong conquers Right, and the black shadow of ill
Covers the earth with drought and drear eclipse,
And stammering prayers are uttered by pale lips,
And Tyrants triumph, and Fiends drink their fill
Of mortal wretchedness, and quick blights kill
Virtue i' th' bud of promise;—wherefore this?
Moans the blind soul, stumbling away from bliss
Through the wide mysteries of the eternal Will;
Why fainteth Love in the rude grasp of Hate?
Why creeps the Genius which hath wings to soar?
And human Misery, fronting human Fate,
Scorn and deny Thee, Father, evermore?
Till even the faithful falter from the dust.
O awful God! *we hope* that thou art just.

THE REVELATION OF DEATH.

II.

"Light! give me light!"[1] — the expiring Poet cried,
Closing his languid eyelids on the day,
And with that solemn cry he passed away;
And haply Doubt was solved, and Error died,
And glimmering Trust was grandly glorified,
Even in the moment of his mightiest need;
And that same light God planteth as a seed,
Outburst from darkness to a broad noontide;
So that *he* saw as, Brothers! *we shall* see
(Freed by the angel Death) the chain sublime
Which binds dim Earth to clear Eternity,
Gleam from the duskiest depths of doubtful Time;
And learnt, as *we shall* learn, the wondrous plan
"Which justifies the ways of God to man."

---

[1] "The last audible words of Goethe were, More Light! The final darkness grew apace, and he, whose eternal longings had been for more Light, gave a parting cry for it as he was passing under the shadow of Death." *Lewes's Life and Works of Goethe,* vol. ii. p. 456.

PRE-EXISTENCE.

If Immortality be not a dream,
Wherefore should we have never known of yore
Another life than ours, a mystic shore,
Whose memory haunts us as a shadowy beam
Of pallid starlight haunts a clouded stream?
What lives for aye hereafter, must before
Have felt the pulse of being; our weak lore
Declares it not; is't therefore the false gleam
Of fantasy, which holds we rise to Heaven
By infinite gradations, through all rounds
Of multiform experience — by the levin
Of fiery trial hallowed in the bounds
Of many worlds, till the immaculate soul
Stands on the heights of Godhead pure and whole?

SONNET.

Too oft the Poet in elaborate verse,
Flushed with quaint images and gorgeous tropes,
Casteth a doubtful light, which is not Hope's,
On the dark spot where Death hath sealed his curse
In monumental silence. Nature starts
Indignant from the sacrilege of words
That ring so hollow, and forlornly girds
Her great woe round her; there's no trick of Art's,
But shows most ghastly by a new-made tomb.
I see no balm in Gilead; he is lost, —
The beautiful soul that loved thee, — thy life's bloom,
Is withered by the sudden blighting frost;
O Grief! how mighty, — Creeds! how vain ye are:
Earth presses closely, — Heaven is cold and far.

ELEGIAC.

I.

"Whom the Gods love, die early,"— it may be,—
But standing, noble Friend, beside thy grave,
Whereon already the lush grasses wave,
Nursed by the pitying Skies' serenity,
[While the pent grief expands, the tears gush free,]
I do arraign the fiery Fate whose blow,
In thy bright morn of years, hath laid thee low,
Whose noon had held all gifts of fame in fee;
Thou wert a Prince in manhood; every grace
Of generous nurture and of genial blood
Beamed in thy presence; and thy lordly face,
The dial of a clear and lofty mood;
Yet now thou art a Phantom,— all is fled,—
The grace, the glory,— God! canst thou be dead?

II.

For aye Thou art before me! day and night,
A ghastly visage, wan and crowned with gore,
Doth haunt my steps and front me evermore,
Darkling between my spirit and the light;
I cannot purge my memory, cleanse my sight;
Blood hovers in the sunbeams; the sweet air
Of the calm evening is no longer fair,
And universal Nature owns the blight:
Alas! what boots it? individual grief,
On the wide ocean of man's common woe,
Shrinks to a current, oh, how vain and brief!
Dwarfed in the height of that eternal flow,
Yet strong to dim Love's joy-illumined eyes,
And shut from Hope the peace of earth and skies.

IMMATURITY.

The fields are ripening to the harvest bloom,
The full grain reddens in the fiery morn,
When, lo! — a mighty whirlwind, sudden-born,
Blights the fair produce with untimely doom; —
Oft do the coral islands faintly loom
Above the South-sea waters, to sink back,
Crumbling to ruin in the earthquake's track,
And what had risen an Eden, rests — a tomb.
Thus, glorious natures, toiling through the years,
Just ready to yield up the glowing flowers
Of faith and genius, fall amid their peers,
And bear to Darkness those supernal powers,
Wrought slowly upward with elaborate care,
Swelling from depths obscure, to fill the loftiest
    Sphere.

SONNET.

He stands as one to whom all life is vain,
And death is terrorless, — the misty dread,
Wherewith the Future veils her awful head,
Hath touched him like the shadow of past pain;
He has no heart to woo Faith's lofty lore,
The aspiring Instincts of his youth have fled,
And even the shining tracks on which they sped
Shall never catch their waning glory more.
O Life! O Sorrow! fare ye well together!
At last Nepenthe comes with healing wings,
And a faint music girds the final sleep;
Alas! he cannot sigh, he cannot weep;
And even the hope this blest deliverance brings,
Falls like a doubtful gleam of Autumn weather.

SONNET.

Between the sunken Sun and the new Moon,
I stood in fields through which a clear brook ran
With scarce perceptible motion, not a span
Of its smooth surface trembling to the tune
Of sunset breezes: "O delicious boon,"
I cried, "of quiet!— wise is Nature's plan,
Who, in her realm, as in the soul of man,
Alternates storm with calm, and the loud Noon
With dewy Evening's soft and sacred lull:
Happy the Heart that keeps *its* twilight hour,
And, in the depths of heavenly peace reclined,
Loves to commune with thoughts of tender power,
Thoughts that ascend,— like Angels beautiful,—
A shining Jacob's ladder of the mind."

SONNET.

A CHARACTER.

A VAIN old man, grasping at worldly hoards,
On the dim verge of threescore years and ten,
Still mingling in the turbid strife of men,
Still struggling for its false and mean rewards,
Mammon and Custom, — his soul's sovereign Lords,
He worships on the grave of health and youth, —
His dull ears closed against the voice of truth,
And warning Wisdom's mild and sweet accords;
Gracious in bearing, generous in great *words*,
By dwarfish *deeds* most impotently crowned,
High in the Paradise of Fools he reigns
'Mid insufficient joys and sordid pains;
But self-assured within that narrow round,
The exalted spirit's nobler faith disdains!

SONNET.

THE GARDEN IN THE CITY.

Here in the City's hot and lurid heart,
Embowered with richest green, the Garden lies
Open to each soft influence of the skies, —
A natural brilliant on the breast of Art,
A shrine for quiet fancies 'mid the Mart,
Whose multiplied harsh tumult faints and dies
Adown its still arcades; here Thought may rise
Above base Mammon worship, and take part
In the soul's inmost drama of delight,
Its play of constant hopes, its prophet-powers,
Half shrouded, yet indued with prescient might,
And bathed with sunshine from far future hours,
Calm Meditation merging faith in sight,
And drooping Will made strong in Nature's secret
    bowers!

SONNET.

O! weary bondage of the clouding clay,
O! prison of base darkness, in whose gloom
Life shows a ghastly spectre, stript of bloom,
And beauty faintly struggles with decay,—
Come Death! with thy kind lightnings, rend away
The crowded shadows, break the charnel doom,
Haunting our years, as vapors haunt a tomb,
Shut from the morning's songs and bliss of day;
Thou Blaster of all hope in hearts of joy,
To *ours* thou shalt be welcome as a Bride
Of passionate eyes and love-enamoured breath;
The shock of thy sharp summons shall destroy
The hideous thrall upon us, and a tide
Of happier Life gush from the stroke of Death.

SONNET.

TO A CELEBRATED ACTRESS.

ALL moods and feelings,— Sorrow, Love, Delight,
Tempestuous Pride, and low-voiced Tenderness,—
The mournful pleadings of a mute Distress,
And regal Passion's fiery-vested might,—
Thou hast embodied to our souls and sight,
Unsealing the deep fountains of our tears,
Or lifting up our spirits from their spheres
In the low ACTUAL to the glorious height
Of some sublime IDEAL;— Art in thee,
The genial handmaid of a natural grace,
Moves to a queenly measure, bold and free,
Yet, moulded ever in each perfect part
By that serene and sweet humanity
Which crowns the genius with the loyal Heart!

SONNET.

WRITTEN ON A FLY-LEAF OF THE LETTERS AND JOURNALS OF SIR HUDSON LOWE, EDITED BY WILLIAM FORSYTH, M. A.

How vain with pleas like *this* to quench the hate,
The righteous hate, which, following hot and fast,
Like an o'ermastering torrent, whelmed at last
The false Malignant!— he who stooped to sate
His bloodless passions on the fallen Great, —
To wound and sting by every pitiful art
That brave, heroic, sorely-smitten heart,
Pierced to the core with deadly shafts of Fate:
Base spirit! one unanimous voice of scorn
Uprose and rang forever in thine ears, —
A haunting voice, reëchoed down the years;
O! thou didst live detested, die forlorn, —
So racked by Memories fierce, by coward Fears,
'Twere best, methinks, that thou hadst ne'er been born!

SONNET.

AFTER THE STORM.

A LONG, wild swell! a waste of turbulent sea,
Thrilled with the storm's last thunders; overhead,
A spectral sky down-glimmering, white and dead,
On the gray billows staring sullenly
Up to the colorless heavens;— the winds so free
But yester-eve, so furious, harsh, and dread,
Have hushed their warring turmoils, and are fled
To ocean-gulfs;— the zephyr's gentle glee
Waits for the lingering sunrise;— while we look,
The clouds, like leaves of some dark-volumed book,
Holding a glorious mystery, roll apart,
A sudden splendor smites the leaden skies,
The waste is all ablaze, the waters start
To rapture 'neath the morning's passionate eyes!

SONNET.

WELL spake the Poet, that howe'er the cry
Of frenzied sorrow might call loud on death,[1]
No soul hath prayed that with our transient breath,
The last sad burden of a mortal sigh,
Life — thought — desire — should perish utterly;
O! rather would the spirit bear the yoke
Of *torture*, if beyond its prison-bars
A glimmer of the feeblest promise broke,
Athwart new heavens, sown thick with happy stars;
O! rather would we hold that doctrine just,
Whereby mankind — save some through Christ set
    free —
Shall writhe for aye divorced from joy and trust,
Than yield up thus our Immortality,
Quenching THAT HOPE in darkness and the dust.

[1] "*Whatever crazy sorrow saith,*
No life that breathes with human breath
Has ever truly longed for death."
                Tennyson's "*Two Voices.*"

SONNET.

DEDICATED TO M. H. H.

Her face is very noble, and her mien
Gracious, and sweet as sunshine; in her eyes
Dwell the deep lights of tender sympathies
Which, from abysses of her soul serene,
Come out like stars from depths of quiet skies
Made lustrous by the night of others' pain;
Her deeds of patient goodness fall like rain
Upon our arid spirits, whence arise
Warm benedictions gladdening all her way
With heavenly music; as her stormy day,
So is her strength; amid earth's bitter woes
The river of her mercy gently flows;
Sick hearts revive, and fading hopes grow green,
And frenzied Passions sink to soft repose.

SONNET.

THE ACTOR TO THE THINKER.

PALE Thinker! wed to Monkish solitude!
Weaving the subtle substance of thy mind
In flimsy webs of speculation blind,
Fearful lest some bold worldling should intrude;
How false the pride of that self-conscious mood,
Wherein thou claim'st the power to loose, or bind
The car of progress; *thou* that liest reclined
At lazy length in depths of vernal wood:
Give ME the pulse of action, the fierce hope
Of triumph 'midst the crowding ranks of men
In mart, or field, or temple; let me cope,
Not with vain *dreams* in some deep-shadowed glen,
But those stern *facts* which conquered, straightway ope
The Gates of Fortune to our eager ken!

SONNET.

ALL day the distant mountain tops have worn
A glory caught from the frank August sun,
Steadfast, serene, unwaning, — all save one
Tall peak o'er which a storm-cloud seems to mourn,
Or, oftener still, to threaten, as its torn
And fiery heart, rent by the lightning bolt,
Gleams with a terrible glare o'er heath and holt,
The desolate mountain caves, and dells forlorn:
Why wreaks the storm its fury on *that* height,
Lonely and rugged, of sweet verdure bared?
Because yon haughty peak alone has dared
To tower above its peers, to grasp the sky; —
Storms, and not sunshine, gird the soul of might,
And barren is all bold supremacy!

SONNET.

The West is one great sea of cloudy fire,
Above the horizon flaming in a flood
Of such thick glory, that the Autumn wood
Towers in the splendor like a burning pyre
Built in the heat of sacrificial ire,
In honor of some fierce Divinity;
Some barbarous God of dreadful brow, and eye
Red with the fumes of slaughter, and the dire
Designs he fosters in his evil might;
It burns, and burns from shadowy mountain base
Slow-smouldering upwards to the loftiest height,
Whereon the feignéd flames with sunset die,
But not in darkness, for the radiant grace
Of Eve, and Eve's calm Planet, shame the Night.

THE PRESENTIMENT.

Over her face, so tender and meek,
  The light of a prophecy lies,
That hath silvered the red of the rose on her
    cheek,
  And chastened the thought in her eyes.

Beautiful eyes, with an inward glance
  To the spirit's mystical deep;
Lost in the languid gleam of a trance,
  More solemn and saintly than sleep.

It hints of a world which is alien and dim,
  Of a nature that hovers between
The discord of earth and the seraphim's hymn,
  On the verge of the spectral — Unseen;

And forever and ever she seems to hear
  The voice of a charmer implore,
" Come! enter the life that is noble and clear;
  Come! grow to my heart once more."

And forever and ever she mutely turns
  From a mortal lover's sighs;
And fainter the red of the rose-flush burns,
  And deeper the thought in her eyes.

The seeds are warm of the churchyard flowers,
  That will blossom above her rest,
And a bird that shall sing by the old church towers,
Is already fledged in its nest.

And so when a blander summer shall smile,
  On some night of soft July,
We will lend to the dust her beauty awhile,
  'Neath the hush of a moonless sky.

And later still shall the churchyard flowers
  Gleam nigh with a white increase;
And a bird outpour, by the old church towers,
  A plaintive poem of peace.

QUEEN GALENA;

OR, THE SULTANA BETRAYED.

HOLD! let the heartless Perjurer go!
Speak not! strike not! he is *my* foe, —
From me, me only, comes the blow, —
I will repay him woe for woe;
Look in my eyes! my eyes are dry,
I breathe no plaint, I heave no sigh,
But — will avenge me ere I die.

Think you that I shall basely rest,
And know the bosom mine hath pressed
Is couched upon a colder breast?
Think you that I shall yield the West,
The Orient soul *my* nature nurst,
Till the black seed of treachery burst,
And blossomed to this deed accurst?

My rival! O! her eyes are meek,
Her faltering presence wan and weak
As the faint flush that tints her cheek;
'Tis not on *her* that I would wreak

My vengeance, — sooner would I wring
Life from an insect-birth of spring
Than palter with so poor a thing.

But He, — I tell you if he flew,
As it was once his wont to do,
Repentant — pleading — quick to woo,
With all his wild heart flaming through
The glance of passion, — it were sweet,
Yea, noble, righteous, just, and meet,
To slay him kneeling at my feet!

He *shall not* wed her; by Heaven's light
He shall not: o'er my lurid sight
Throbs a thick fire; the ancient might
Of a stern race is stirred to-night;
My sovereign claim annul — disown!
I will repay him groan for groan,
Or — stab him at the altar-stone!

"THE WINTER WINDS MAY WILDLY RAVE."

The winter Winds may wildly rave,
    Lost Edith, o'er thy place of rest;
But, love! thou hast a holier grave
    Deep in a faithful human breast.

There, the Embalmer, Memory, bends,
    Watching, with softly-breathèd sighs,
The mystic light her genius lends
    To fadeless cheeks, and tender eyes.

There, in an awful calm serene,
    Thy beauty keeps its saintly trace,
The radiance of an angel mien,
    The rapture of a heavenly grace.

And there, O! gentlest Love remain,
    (No stormy passion round thee raves,)
Till, soul to soul, we meet again
    Beyond this ghostly realm of graves.

LINES

ON THE DEATH OF THE REV. J. A. S., THE DISTINGUISHED PASTOR OF THE CHURCH OF ST. PETER, CHARLESTON, S. C.

As those who, sailing in a Tropic Sea,
Through golden calms borne on contentedly,
And yielded to a listless noonday sleep,
Are roused therefrom by thunder on the Deep,
And wake to sudden turmoil and the dread
Of lightning, which has struck a comrade dead,
(Their faithful Pilot laboring at the wheel,)
O! thus we slumbered, and thus burst the peal
Of death's artillery, and the bolt of woe
Which smote *his* noble Life, and laid it mute and
    low.

Our souls were still — our lives, a summer sea —
When the great God, who worketh fearfully,
Around whose will the shroud of mystery's thrown,
Whose paths are dim, whose footsteps are not known,

Wrapped in the awful cloud, and darkness came,
And on our shuddering hearts his judgment wrote in
    flame.

But what, to our weak sight, is girt about
With mist of grief and chilling shades of doubt,
To him we mourn is very bright and clear, —
His is the joy, and OURS the blight and fear;
His the vast freedom, ours the prison wall;
His the white robe, and ours the bier and pall;
His the calm Height which overtops the spheres,
And ours the Depth of passionate despairs;
Then should we for ourselves and children keep
The bitter human tears 'tis vain for him to weep.

But tears must fall, and sorrowing words be spoken,
And stricken hearts lament, or else — be broken;
'Tis not 'mid bleeding love's late-severed ties,
We thrill to feel the healing Comfort rise,
And catch the inner hymns of Paradise, —
Gently, and as the morn from banks of gloom
Is slowly rounded upward into bloom,
That tender Angel steals upon our being,
And with it comes a harmony, agreeing
With the soft sunshine of its heavenly spell,
And startled Faith returns, and all is well.

Then, from the cypress gloom, the darkening sod,
We lift our eyes to the pure light of God,
Where 'mid the shining ranks, absolved from sin,
A perfect spirit hath just entered in,
Felt the keen rapture of its last release,
Received the immortal Crown, and clasped the palm
 of Peace.

THE BATTLE IN THE DISTANCE.

HER dark eyes gleamed amid the gloom,
 Slow gathering from the stormy main,
She stood as one who fronts her doom,
 And tasks the mystic Fate in vain:
Sudden, a steed with drooping rein,
 Burst from the desert's shadowy rim,
And flecked with many a crimson stain,
 Paused by the portal, black and grim.

She knew the steed, — she marked the cloud
 Which rolled across the distant fight,
And strove to pierce the awful shroud, —
 But a strange mist o'erhung her sight,
The prospect swayed in doubtful light,
 And, idly tottering to and fro,
She shivered 'neath the lurid might
 Of prescient Thoughts foreboding woe.

"O, Love! last eve, your head was laid
 Close to this warm and tender breast,
And all the thrilling vows we made,
 And all I knew, and all I *guessed*,

Of passion breathed, or unexprest,
  Did point to bliss built up on bliss,
An Aidenne of voluptuous rest
  New-opened by each burning kiss.

"But Fate is stern, and men are base,
  Wrong creepeth in the dark to smite, —
A caitiff who had seen my face
  Once — on El Kalim's castled height,
Swore by the Houris' brows of light
  To bear me through his Harem gate,
And yonder strives my Roland's right
  With jealous fraud and desperate hate."

But see! the cloud rolls up apace!
  But hark! the shouts grow wild and clear!
A sudden whirlwind! and the place
  Of strife looms outward everywhere; —
And lo! his proud plume waved in air,
  The victor Roland! — a dense throng
With glittering casque, and gleaming spear,
  Shouting an ancient knightly song

Of triumph, close around their Lord,
  And banners flaunt, and trumpets peal,
And thundering on the level sward
  Rush the fierce chargers, clad in steel;

The solid feudal bastions reel,
    The welkin thrills to brave alarms,
Tumultuous liegemens' fiery zeal,
    With clang of hoofs, and clash of arms.

That night the bonfires hid the stars,
    The mighty wassail bowl foamed high,
And to the deepest dungeon-bars,
    Rang the uproarious revelry;
And knights did woo, and ladies sigh,
    And minstrels sung, and jesters laughed,
And gayly sped from eye to eye,
    Love winged his fairy-feathered shaft.

But in a cloister near the sea,
    Shut from the jest, the dance, the tale,
While the low winds breathe mournfully,
    And shadows throng, and billows wail,
Bowed by the altar, hushed and pale,
    The Lord and Lady court the calm,
Till the last lingering echoes fail
    Of solemn prayer and saintly psalm!

TO A FRIEND IN AFFLICTION.

Oh! bitter is this final blow!
Yet shouldst thou strive to battle still,
To calm the heart, to nerve the will,
   And overcome the woe;—

Although thou walk'st a desolate path,
Where all the blooms of life *seem* dead,
And fierce, and threatening overhead,
   The thunder speaks in wrath;—

Yet never, while the sovereign brain
Retains the rule by Nature given,
Should misery shake our trust in heaven,
   Or Manhood crouch to Pain!

Young art thou, and this stormy day,
So cold, so dim, so cheerless now,
May thrill thy brightening soul and brow
   With sudden noontide ray;—

Or else, ere Life shall sink to Night,
A golden sunset-calm may rise,
To flush thy spirit's peaceful skies
  With blessed evening light.

Whate'er betide, 'tis noblest, best,
Against all earthly ills to cope,
Keep to the last our heart and hope,
  And leave with God the rest!

THE SOUL-CONFLICT.

I.

DEFEATED! but never disheartened!
   Repulsed! but unconquered in will, —
Upon dreary discomfitures building
   Her virtue's strong battlements still,
The SOUL, through the siege of Temptations,
   Yields not unto Fraud, nor to Might,
Unquelled by the rush of the Passions,
   Serene 'mid the tumults of fight.

II.

She sees a grand prize in the distance,
   She hears a glad sound of acclaims,
The crown wrought of blooms Amaranthine,
   The music far sweeter than Fame's.
And so, 'gainst the rush of the Passions
   She lifts the broad buckler of Right,
And so, through the glooms of Temptation,
   She walks in a splendor of light.

LIFE'S UNDER-CURRENT.

Mankind esteemed him happy! filled with good
    Of all things grateful unto youth's desire;
Alas! they neither saw, nor understood
    His sorrow's secret fire.

How could they dream that one whose genial face
    Seemed the sure index of a soul at rest,
Watched in the darkening shadow of disgrace,
    Fierce torture in his breast?

How could they tell that one whose smiles would wake
    To such quick radiance of responsive glee,
Unseen tormentors to a viewless stake
    Had bound in agony?

O, shallow wisdom of this world, avaunt!
    Thou seest the outward show, the whited tomb,
But there is that within would stir and daunt,
    And shake thee as with doom!

Mirth, silvery clear, from breaking hearts may rise,
  Gay laughter quiver upon Misery's lips,
'Tis not the whimpering soul that shrinks and sighs,
  That most has known eclipse;—

For strong hearts, strong in joy, more strong in pain,
  Dare to the last the banded hosts of Fate,
And covering o'er their death-wounds, on the plain,
  Sink even in death elate.

We cannot mould our lives, but can our wills
  Gird with keen-steeled resolve to meet our foes,
And he who fights unyielding — *he* fulfils
  A doom to which repose,

The sordid quiet of your sensual souls
  Is mean and tame, as those low lands which lie
'Twixt mountain peaks that swell the thunder-rolls,
  The battling eagle's cry.

SONG.

Fly, swiftly fly
  Through yon fair sky,
 O purple-pinioned Hours!
And bring once more the balmy night,
When from her lattice, silvery bright,
Love's beacon star — her taper — shines
Between those dark manorial pines,
  Above the myrtle bowers.

Fly, breezes, fly,
  And waft my sigh
 With love's warm fondness fraught,
'Twill stir my lady's languid mood,
Where, in her verdurous solitude,
She sits and thinks, — a moonlight grace
Cast o'er her beauteous brow and face,
  Touched by a passionate thought!

Glide, rivulet, glide
  With whispering tide,
 Through coverts lone and deep,

To woo her with the airy call,
The music faint, the far-off fall
Of fairy streams in fairy climes,
Or pleasant lapse of fairy rhymes,
   Soft as her breath in sleep.

   Fly, swiftly fly
    Through yon calm sky,
 O tremulous-breasted dove!
And pausing on her favorite tree,
Murmur your plaint so tenderly,
That, born of that deep tone, a charm
Her very heart of hearts may warm
   With rosy bliss of love.

   Fly, swiftly fly
    Through yon fair sky,
 O purple-pinioned Hours!
And bring once more the balmy night,
When from her lattice, silvery bright,
Love's beacon star — her taper — shines
Between those dark manorial pines
   Above the myrtle bowers!

SONG.

I.

Here, long ago,
While the fair River in its spring-time flow,
    Murmured with happy voice
    "Rejoice! Rejoice!"
While youth's full pulses thrilled within our breasts,
Far from life's hopeless calms, or fierce unrests,
    We told our love;
The April sunset heaven was bright above,
    The earth below
Most beautiful — but this was long ago,
    Long, very long ago.

II.

Here, once again,
While the dark River like a soul in pain
Heaves, as it were from depths of human care,
    A sigh of lorn despair;
Youth's glorious pulses stilled within our breasts,
The haunt of hopeless calms, or fierce unrests,

We speak — but NOT of love!
The angry winter's heaven is wild above,
    The earth below
Drear as the hopes that withered long ago,
    Long, very long ago.

SONG.

Ho! fetch me the winecup! fill up to the brim!
For my heart has grown cold, and my vision is dim,
And I fain would bring back for a moment the glow,
The swift passion that age has long chilled with its snow;—
Ho! fetch me the winecup! the red liquor gleams,
With a promise to waken youth's rapture of dreams,
And I'll drain the bright draught for that promise divine,
Though Death, Death the Spectre, should hand me the wine.

'Tis not life that I live, for the blood-currents glide
Through my wan shrunken veins in so sluggish a tide,
That my heart droops and withers; what! *life* call you this?
O! rather, consumed by one keen thrill of bliss,

SONG.

Would I die with youth's glory revivified round me,
The deep eyes that blessed, and the white arms that bound me;
O! rather than brood in this dusk of desire,
Sink down, like yon gorgeous sunset, all fire,
The soul clad with wings, and the brain steeped in light;—
Then come, potent Wizard! I call on thy might,
Breathe a magical mist o'er the ravage of Time,
Roll back the sad years to the flush of my prime,
And I'll drain thy bright draught for that vision divine,
Though Death, Death the Spectre, should hand me the wine!

SONG OF THE NAIADS.

Gay is our crystal floor
    Beneath the wave,
With strange gems flaming o'er,
    The Genii gave;
Sweet is the purple light
That haunts our happy sight,
And low and sweet the lulling strains that sigh
While the tides pause, and the faint zephyrs die —

Come! come! and seek us here,
    In these cool deeps,
Where all is calmly fair,
    And sorrow sleeps:
Thy burning brow shall rest,
Couched on a tender breast,
And, charmed to bliss, thy soul shall catch the gleams
Of mystic glories in ambrosial dreams.

Come! for the earth is drear,
    The tempests rave,

And the fast-failing year
   Is nigh its grave:
Thy summer, too, is passed,
   Wouldst thou have peace at last?
O! here she dwells serenely in still caves,
And waits to woo thee underneath the waves.

PALINGENESIS.

I DREAMED of late a mystic dream!
　Methought that Death
Had struck my heart's warm pulses still,
　And robbed my breath:

This feverish blood, and troubled soul
　Were calm and cold;
That which *had* borne thought, passion, will,
　Was — senseless mould;

I saw the mourners round my bed —
　I heard their wail;
I knew what heavy tear-storms drenched
　My forehead pale:

Yet — I was dead, dead, dead, for aye!
　My blood was ice,
And crumbled with my crumbling brain
　Thought's last device.

They bore me to a lone churchyard —
    The eve was mild,
Save that a strange wind weirdly sung
    Its requiem wild.

Months, years, and centuries lapsed away,
    In dead repose:
Sudden, my lifeless ashes stirred
    With feeblest throes!

A dim, dull sense crept struggling through
    My palsied frame,
And flickering from the formless void,
    A pallid flame,

Awoke, methought, one little seed,
    Whose latent germ
Burst through the cerement's mouldering folds,
    And scorned the worm:

It grew, it spread, it towered to heaven!
    A mighty oak,
Proof 'gainst the fiercest tempest-wrath,
    The levin's stroke!

But when spring-breezes blew, its boughs
    Such music made,

Men deemed that hid in murmurous green,
  Wood-fairies played:

They knew not that a poet-soul,
  For ages flown,
Thrilled the warm leaves to whispering song,
  Or — mystic moan!

THE BROOK.

But yesterday this brook was bright,
And tranquil as the clear moonlight,
That woos the palms on Orient shores,
But now, a hoarse, dark stream, it pours
Impetuous o'er its bed of rock,
And almost with a thunder-shock
Boils into eddies, fierce and fleet,
That dash the white foam round our feet,
A raging whirl of waters, rent
As if with angry discontent!

A tempest in the night swept by,
Born of a murk and fiery sky,
And while the solid woodlands shook,
It wreaked its fury on the brook.
The evil genius of the blast
Within its quiet bosom passed,
And therefore is it that a tide,
Which used as lovingly to glide
As thoughts through spirits sanctified,
Rolls now a whirl of waters, rent
As if with angry discontent.

I knew, of late, a creature, bright
And gentle as the clear moonlight,
The tenderest, and the kindest heart
God ever sent a loving part
To act on earth, across whose life
A sudden passion swept, in strife,
With wild, unhallowed forces rife.
It stirred her nature's inmost deep,
That nevermore shall rest' or sleep;
Remorse, its rugged bed of rock,
O'er which for aye, with thunder-shock,
The tides of feeling, fierce and fleet,
Are dashed to foam or icy sleet,
A raging whirl of waters, rent
By something worse than discontent!

THE POET'S TRUST IN HIS SORROW.

I.

O God! how sad a doom is mine,
  To human seeming;
Thou hast called on me to resign
So much — much! — *all* — but the divine
  Delights of dreaming.

II.

I set my dreams to music wild,
  A wealth of measures;
My lays, thank Heaven! are undefiled,
I sport with Fancy as a child
  With golden leisures.

III.

And long as Fate, not wholly stern,
  But this shall grant me,
Still with perennial faith to turn
Where Song's unsullied Altars burn,
  Nought, nought shall daunt me!

IV.

What though my worldly state be low
  Beyond redressing;
I own an inner Flame whose glow
Makes radiant all the outward snow;
  My last great blessing!

LINES.

COMPOSED UPON A BEAUTIFUL DAY IN AUTUMN.

How grandly in the mild September rays
Rest the rich forests, and the cloudless sky!
Thou queenliest of the regal Autumn days,
Would that thy happy Hours might never fly!

O! that the same calm glory in the air
Might bless forevermore our grateful sight!
O! that the Earth might ever seem as fair
And Nature wear for aye these robes of light!

In the still Present, musing, let me rest,
The Past be banished, and the Future veiled!
Dark fears! yield up your empire in my breast,
Fierce memories! leave my spirit unassailed:

This genial morn I give to gentle thought,
Angels of peace and comfort hover nigh;
Sweet Hope, so long an alien, comes unsought,
And Joy resumes her sway, I know not why:

Yet, Heaven! I thank thee for these healthful
 gleams
Of present bliss, though brief the rapture be;
They pierce the sullen darkness of my dreams,
They bring me near — oh! Father! — unto thee!

THE TEMPTER IN THE HOUSE.

The sky is dark with a cloudy pall,
    And the earth is dim with rain,
And the ghastly pine trees toss and moan
    By the side of the moaning main;
And around the eaves of the desolate Hall
    The shrill March winds complain.

But a darker pall has shrouded the light
    Of the Household Hopes within,
For the troubled hearts that toss and moan
    By the terrible verge of sin
Are sorely beset by the Tempter's might,
    And the Devil is sure to win!

THE UNPRISONED SPIRITS.

Our prison walls are wrecked and gray;
　　Cast not a glance behind us,
For forceful fraud has ceased to stay,
　　And tyrant chains to bind us;
Press onward where his herald-gleams
　　The Day-God sends in warning,
Shake off the Léthean dew of dreams,
　　And speed to hail the morning;
Dreary the night, and foul the wrong
　　That curbed our bold endeavor,
But though the despot held us long,
　　He could not hold forever.

Brave hearts, and high in Hell's despite
　　Can ne'er make base surrender
Of THAT which clothes the will with might,
　　The Genius with its splendor;
The Gods of earth may tempt and blind
　　The souls that soar above them,
But worthier Fates will seek, and find,
　　And nobler Masters prove them;

So, when the Tempter's hour is passed,
   His bonds are rent asunder,
His dungeon topples in the blast,
   And falls before the thunder.

Then rise the souls he could not tame
   To write — in *deeds* — their story;
To pluck the laurel-wreath from Fame,
   And scale the Mount of Glory;
Then, stronger for the deep disgust
   Of brief revolt from Duty,
They fight the battle of the Just,
   Led on by Truth and Beauty;
Upborne from sun-crowned height to height,
   They chase the grand Ideal
Till conquering faith is merged in sight,
   The IDEAL in the REAL!

THE CONDEMNED.

A FRAGMENT.

The night is dim, the starry watch-fires fail,
The boding clouds troop by in spectral guise,
The embers on our cheerless hearth are pale,
And sweet! I cannot see thy loving eyes;
I only *feel* them burning through the gloom,
I only know thy loving presence nigh
By the low burden of a prescient sigh,
    Forerunning my sad doom.

Draw near my love, and let me clasp once more,
Once more, and for the last, last time on earth,
Thy stainless hand; mine own is dark with gore,
And yet, thou shrink'st not; Danger, Doubt, and Dearth
The tempest of thy mighty love hath swept
Back from the path through which our Fates have led,
And though to-morrow's eve shall find me dead,
    I shall not sleep — unwept!

ON A PORTRAIT.

The face, the beautiful face,
   In its living flush and glow,
The perfect face in its peerless grace
   That I worshipped long ago;
That I worshipped when youth was strong and bold,
   That I worship now,
Though the pulse of youth grows faint and low,
   And the ashes of hope are cold.

The face, the beautiful face,
   Ever haunting my heart and brain,
Bringing ofttimes a dream of heaven,
   Ofttimes the pang of a pain
Which darteth down like a lightning flash
   To the dreadful deeps,
Where the gems of a shipwrecked life are cast,
   And its dead — cold promise sleeps.

Sweet face! shall I meet thee again,
   In the peaceful land of palms,
By the banks of the rainbow-crownéd streams,
   In the hush of the heavenly calms?

Or, forever and ever and evermore,
    While the years depart,
    While the ages roll,
Walk the glooms of a ghostly shore,
    In the fear of a phantom-haunted brain,
    And a cloud-encircled soul —
With a haunted brain, and a cheerless heart,
    While the years and the ages roll?

No answer comes to my cry,
    Though out of the depths I call:
Not the faintest gleam of a hopeful beam
    Shines over the shroud and pall.
My soul is clothed with sackcloth and dust,
    And I look from my widowed hearth
      With a vacant eye on the tumult and stir
    Of this weary, dreary earth —
For my soul is dead and its hopes are dust,
And the joy of passion, the strength of trust,
    These passed from the world with HER.

SUNSET AND MOONLIGHT.

HERE, glancing from this breezy Height,
While the still Day goes slowly down,
And sombre Evening's shadows brown
Close o'er the purple-flushing light,

I mark the softer radiance rest
Of the calm moon, till now unseen,
Along the Ocean tides serene,
Scarce heaving toward the faded West;

At first there dawns a ghostly ray,
Faint as a new-born infant's dreams,
But soon an ampler glory streams,
And trembling up the lustrous Bay,

Long level shafts of silvery glow
Lead upward to the quiet skies,
The radiant paths to Paradise
Revealed when all is dark below.

THE TWO SUMMERS.

There is a golden season in our year
Between October's hale and lusty cheer
And the hoar frost of Winter's empire drear,

Which, like a fairy flood of mystic tides
Whereon divine Tranquillity abides,
The kingdom of the sovereign Months divides:

Then wailing Autumn winds their requiems cease,
Ere Winter's sturdier storms have gained release,
And earth and heaven alike are bright with peace.

O Soul! thou hast thy golden season too!
A blissful interlude of birds, and dew,
Of balmy gales, and skies of deepest blue!

That *second Summer* when thy work is done,
The harvest hoarded, and the Autumn sun
Gleams on the fruitful fields thy toil hath won;

Which, also, like a fair mysterious tide
Whereon calm Thoughts like ships at anchor ride,
Doth the broad Empire of thy years divide.

This passed, what more of life's brief path remains
Winds through unlighted vales, and dismal plains,
The haunt of chilling Blights, or fevered Pains.

Pray then, ye happy few along whose way
Life's Indian Summer pours its mellow ray,
That ye may die ere dawns the Evil Day;

Sink on that Season's kind and genial breast,
While Peace and Sunshine rule the cloudless West,
The elect of God whom Life and Death have blessed.

THE ISLAND IN THE SOUTH.

THE Ship went down at noonday in a calm,
When not a zephyr broke the crystal sea.
We two escaped alone: we reached an Isle
Whereon the waters settled languidly
In a long swell of music; luminous skies
O'erarched the place, and lazy, broad lagoons
Swept inland, with the boughs of plantain trees
Trailing cool shadows through the dense repose;
All round about us floated gentle airs,
And odors that crept upward to the sense
Like delicate pressures of voluptuous thought.
I, with a long bound, leapt upon the shore
Shouting, but she, pavilioned in dark locks,
Sobbed out thanksgiving; 'twixt the world and us,
Distance that seemed Eternity outrolled
Its terrible barriers; on the waste a Fate
Stood up, and stretching his blank hands abroad
Muttered of desolation. Did we weep,
And groaning cast our foreheads in the dust?
So it *had* been, but in each other's eyes
Smiled a new world, dearer than that which rose

Beneath the lost stars of the faded West.
That very morn the white-stoled priest of God
Had blessed us with the church's choicest prayers,
And these did gird us like a sapphire wall
When the floods threatened, and the ghastly Doom
Moaned itself impotent; free we were to love
To the full scope of passion; a few suns,
And in the deep recesses of the woods
We built ourselves a palace; the dim spot
Was fortressed by the Tropic's giant growths,
Luxuriant Titans of a hundred years;
And the vines, laced and interlaced between,
Drooped with a flowery largess many-hued.
It was a place of Faëry; songs of birds
That glimmered in and out among the leaves,
Like magical dreams embodied, wooed the Winds
To gentlest motion of benignant wings;
And the sun veiled his radiance, and the stars
Peered through the shadowy stillness with a light
So spiritual, the forest seemed to wane
In tremulous lines waved down the silvery aisles.
There lived, there loved we, as none else have lived
And loved since the primeval Blight
Rained down its discords, and death clenched the curse.
No shallow mockeries of a worn-out age,

Effete and helpless, bound young passion round
With the cold fetters of detested forms:
Civilization was not there to set
Its specious seal of custom on our hearts,
Prisoning the bolder virtues; we might dare
To act, speak, think, as the true nature moved,
Untutored and majestic; our souls grew
To the stature of the spirit that looks down
From the unpolluted regnancy of heavens
That hold no curses; the glad universe
Showered rare benedictions on our path;
Matter was merged in poesy; the winds
From the serene Pacific, the quick gales
From mountainous ridges in the uppermost air,
The eternal chorus of far seas forlorn,
The harmony of forests, the small voice
That trembled from the happy rivulet's breast,
All touched us with that sweet philosophy,
Which, if we woo the visible world aright,
Blesses experience with new gates of sense
Wherethrough we gain — Elysium —

      So the years
Were winged and odorous with a thousand joys,
Of which the poor slave to the hollow law
We term society, hath had no dream;
Our love was comprehensive, full, divine,
Rounding the perfect orbit wherein life

Should gravitate to God, even as the spheres
Roll to the central fire; love mastered life
As maelstroms suck still waters; love — the one
Electric current through act, reason, will,
Throbbing like inspiration; no vain touch
Of weak, fantastic passion, no thin glow
Of morbid longing, fluttering feebly up
From shallow brains, stirred to a dubious flame,
And tortured with false throes of sentiment —
(That bastard whimperer to the deity — Love —
As a changeling to the Titans) — no red heat
Of base desire, fusing the delicate thought
To chaos; but a steadfast, genial sun,
A luminous glory, gentle as intense,
Making our fate a heaven of warmth, light, rest,
Whose very clouds were halos, and whose storms
Were tempered into music. Thus Time stole
On muffled wings through the still air of bliss,
Gathering our ripened hopes, and sowing seeds
Of joys to come. My innocent bud had flowered
To beauty — oh! such beauty as these lips,
Touched though they were with fire, might not profane
With shackles of mean utterance. Oh, God! God!
Why didst thou take her from me? why transform
The passionate presence in my shielding arms
To this poor phantom of a broken brain,

Mocking my woe with shadows? On a night
When the still sea was calmest, the bright stars
Most bright, and a warm breathing on the wind
Spoke of perpetual Summer, a strange voice
I could not hear, said: "It is evening time,"
And a wan hand my eyes were blind to note
Beckoned her far away —

      The awful grief
Closed round me like an ocean. I was mad,
And raved my memory from me. When again
The world dawned, as a dreary landscape dawns
Grotesquely through the sluggish mists of March —
I walked once more in a great Capital's streets,
A savage 'midst the civilized — a man —
Shattered and wrecked, I grant you — still A
 MAN
Amongst the puppets that usurp the name
And act the fraud so basely, that the Fiend
Wearies to death the echoes of his hell
In laughing at them. I *am* with you still,
Emasculate denizens of the stifling mart,
Where heaven's free winds are throttled in the
 fumes
Of furnaces, and the insulted Sun
Glooms through the crowding vapors at mid-day,
Like a God, re-collecting to himself
His immortality; where nerveless limbs

Bear nerveless bodies to their separate dens
Of torture, and lean, wild-eyed Revellers
Foster the hungering worm that never dies,
And fan the lurid fire unquenchable;
Where stealthy avarice lurks in wait to sack
The widow's house, and license of low minds,
Loaded with prurient knowledge, and — no hearts,
(Self-worship having killed them,) make the world
A Pandemonium. I *am* with you still,
But the hours creep on to a more fortunate time;
A vessel thrills her broad sails in the bay,
And the breeze bloweth seaward; I will seek
My island in the southern waves again;
A thousand memories urge me, tones that slept
Waken to invitation; I can feel
The Hesperian beauty of that realm of peace
Flushing my brain, and fancy; but through all
The ruddy vision *glides a tender shade,*
And pauses with mute meaning by — *a grave.*

THE VILLAGE BEAUTY.

The glowing tints of a Tropic eve
   Burn on her radiant cheek,
And we know that her voice is rich and low,
   Though we never have heard her speak;—
So full are those gracious eyes of light,
   That the blissful flood runs o'er,
And wherever her tranquil pathway tends
   A glory flits on before!

O! very grand are the city belles,
   Of a brilliant and stately mien,
As they walk the steps of the languid dance,
   And flirt in the pause between;
But beneath the boughs of the hoary oak,
   Where the minstrel fountains play,
I think that the artless village girl
   Is sweeter by far than they.

THE VILLAGE BEAUTY.

O! very grand are the city belles,
    But their hearts are worn away
By the keen-edged world, and their lives have lost
    The beauty, and mirth of May;
They move where the sun and the starry dews
    Reign not; they are haughty and bold,
And they do not shrink from the cursèd mart
    Where Faith is the slave of Gold.

But the starry dews and the genial sun
    Have gladdened her guileless youth,
And her brow is bright with the flush of hope,
    Her soul with the seal of truth;
Her feet are beautiful on the hills
    As the steps of an Orient morn,
And Ruth was never more fair to see
    I' the midst of the Autumn corn.

*   *   *   *   *   *   *   *

Dear Effie! give me thy loyal hand,
    As soft and warm as thy heart,
And tell me again I may call thee mine,
    When the winter storms depart;
'Tis true that thou mak'st all seasons bright,
    But is it not fitter that we
Should wed when the Spring — thy sister — comes
    To be a bridesmaid to thee?

The buds will blossom as bloom our hopes,
    And the earth make glad replies
To the music that moves our inmost souls
    With its marvellous harmonies;
And between the Nature that glows without
    And the nature that thrills within,
The delicate morning of love shall close,
    And its bountiful noon begin!

FLOWERS FROM A GRAVE.

These flowers are withered, Lady! like the hopes
We buried in the grave from which they sprung;
Yet are the tokens precious; they have voices,
And sad, sad memories of the broken Past;—
O! I could steep them in my bitter tears,
But that the channels of my grief are closed,
And dryer than their petals; those whose hearts
Have wept blood, seldom find their eyelids moist
With dew of milder sorrow;— from her grave
You plucked these blooms in the soft summer
    dawn;—
Her grave, whose mould lies heavier on our souls
Than e'er on her sweet body; God in Heaven
Reward you for the pure impulsive pity
To which I owe these treasures;— they are dear
To memory as to passion, and though dead,
Are greener than the sapless barren life
Of him who wears them, henceforth, next his heart!

BOUGHT AND SOLD.

I HAVE no hope, and I will not cope
  Base knave with you!—
A Nabob whose gold remains untold,
  What may *I* do to vanquish you,
    And to lift my Love
    To a heart above
The bitter, the cruel, the dazzling spell
Which has snared her soul with the snare of Hell?

  Win her, and wear!
Go to the shrine with a Satyr's leer,
  To the holy altar of God
With the vilest thought that the prurient clod,
  Miscalled your *Heart*, can engender;
    O! guardian Angels, behold and weep!—
  No more in your prayers befriend her,—
For lo! her purity seems to fall
Like a garment off by the chancel wall,
    She is yours to keep
      No more,—
For a woman, a woman, that's bought and sold
In a mart where the Devil pays down the gold,
    Goes forth from the sacred door!

PERFECT CALM.*

Eternal Quiet were eternal sleep!
"O! we will make," some fond Enthusiast cries,
"This present weary world a Paradise
O'er which all gentle Thoughts their watch shall keep;
A noiseless calm shall brood above its bowers,
And only Nature's sweet, and tender powers,
Hold genial converse in the charmèd shade;"

Through the new Eden's golden gates I look,
And lo! stretched listless by a murmuring brook,
Whose silvery lustre glimmers 'mid the glade,
I see the angel Tenant of the place,
Fast by the tree of Life, his placid face
Half hidden in his pinions' downy deep,
The Angel muses, or perchance — he prays! —
Not so, look closer, —— *he is sound asleep!*

* See Thorndale, or the Conflict of Opinions, p. 413.

CHARLOTTE BRONTË.

Through the deep shadows of the darkening years,
She strove with griefs, which oft were agonies, —
The traitorous Hopes transformed to haunting Fears,
The transient Raptures ending but in sighs:

Till at the last, the life-clouds cleared away,
The future bathed in promise heavenly bright,
She heard a tender voice which seemed to say,
"*At evening time, behold! I give thee light!*"

For love, true love, her woman's nature yearned, —
And now true Love hath crowned her longing wild,
And all without, and all within her burned
The glory of his Godhead undefiled.

A new world dawned upon her; divine forms
Gleamed in the sunset on her earnest eyes,
And throned above the years which set in storms,
She saw the opening gates of Paradise;

An earthly Eden, freed from earth's alloy;
Across the happy porch her footsteps passed,
When on the very threshold of her joy,
Death's sudden angel blew his trumpet blast:

The gates of light, as that fierce trumpet rang,
Dissolved, like some vain phantom of the air,
And born of desolation deep, outsprang
A passionate cry — the last — of her despair:

"*Love! we have been so happy! Must we part?*"*
Even as she spoke the final darkness came,
To many sorrowing, and one broken heart,
Leaving thenceforth but memory, and — a name!

* These words, or words to this effect, were the last which Charlotte Brontë uttered.

FRAGMENT OF AN ODE ON THE DEATH OF A GREAT STATESMAN.

Toll forth, O mournful bells, the solemn dirge;
  Speak out to the hushed heavens your lamentation,
A deep funereal music, surge on surge,
  Timed to the sorrow of a stricken Nation;
    For a grand Life hath set,
The last Star in a glorious sky gone down,
And sullen shades of lowering darkness frown,
    Where constellated lights of genius met
On the proud summits of our old Renown!

LETHE.

A DUMB, dark region through whose desolate heart
Creeps a dull river with a stagnant flood;
Its skies are sombre-hued, and dreary clouds,
No wind hath ever stirred, hang low and dim
Above the barren woodlands; all things droop
In slumber; the lithe willow stoops to kiss
The waves, but not a ripple murmurs back
Its salutation, and wan starlike flowers
Yield a white radiance to the failing sense,
And odors pregnant with the charm of rest,
And glamour of Oblivion; all things droop
In slumber; for whate'er hath passed the bounds
Of this miraculous kingdom, — bird or beast, —
Men lured from action, or soul-sick of life,
Weary and heartsore, maids in love's despair,
Or mothers stricken by their first-born's crime, —
All sink without a struggle to deep peace.
Prone in the gleam the river casts abroad,
— A gleam more pallid than the light of Hades, —
Lie those who sought this region ages since;
Their upturned brows are smooth, and tranced
    with calm,

And on their shadowy lips a waning smile
Fitfully glimmers; — round them, rest the forms
Of savage beasts; the Lion all unnerved,
Timid and passionless, his huge limbs relaxed,
And curved to lines of beauty; the fierce Pard
Tamed to a breathless quiet, whilst afar,
Dim seen, but still a HORROR in the Shade,
Gloom the gaunt shapes of mighty brutes of Eld,
The world's primeval tenants; all things droop
In slumber; even the sluggish River's flow
Sounds like the dying surges of the sea
To ears far inland, or the feeblest sigh
Of winds that faint on lofty mountain-tops.
This is the realm — "Oblivion" — this the stream
Which mortals have called — "LETHE!"

JANUARY TO MAY.

I have naught to give thee, lady,—
    Love nor gold;
This dull urn of burial-ashes,
    This is all I hold.

Wouldst thou wed a soul in ruin,
    Clasp a breast,
Where in depth of doubt and darkness
    Bides a demon-guest?

Wouldst thou pour a fervid torrent,
    Passion's flood,
On a wrecked and lonely nature,
    Chilled in brain and blood?

O, forbear! thou wert not fated
    Thus to yield;—
All thy warmth of love and beauty
    Leaves me unannealed.

Plant thy roses in the spring-mould,
  Not the snow;
And thy precious heart-seeds scatter
  Where the seeds may grow!

A REMEMBRANCE.

Softly shone thy lustrous eyes
On that silent summer night,
Softly on my wakened heart,
Thrilling into love and light,
Though from the near mountain's height
The shadows wrapt us solemnly.

Faintly fell the tremulous tones
From thy sweet lips coyly won, —
Dropping with the liquid lull
Of low rivulets, by the sun
Courted from the woodlands dun,
Into pastures, glad and free.

Through the mazes of deep speech
Wandered we, absorbed, — apart, —
On the mingled flood of thought
Drawing nigh each other's heart, —
Till we felt the pulses start
Of a mystic sympathy!

Ah! those brief, harmonious hours!
When their wingéd music fled,
Discord through all voices ran,
And the universe seemed dead,
Only,— moaning o'er its bed,
I heard the low pathetic sea.

THE SHADOW.

The pathway of his mournful life hath wound
   Beneath a Shadow; just beyond it play
   The genial breezes, and the cool brooks stray
Into melodious gushings of sweet sound,
   Whilst ample floods of mellow sunshine fall
   Like a mute rain of rapture over all.

Oft hath he deemed the spell of darkness lost,
   And shouted to the Dayspring; a full glow
   Hath rushed to clasp him, but the subtle Woe
Unvanquished ever, with the might of frost
   Regains its sad realm, and with voice malign
   Saith to the dawning Joy — "This Life is mine!"

Still smiles the brave Soul, undivorced from Hope,
   And, with unwavering eye and warrior mien,
   Walks in the Shadow dauntless and serene,
To test through hostile Years the utmost scope
   Of man's endurance, constant to essay
   All heights of Patience free to feet of clay.

Still smiles the brave Soul undivorced from Hope!
  But now methinks the pale Hope gathers strength,
  Glad winds invade the Silence, streams at length
Flash through the desert; 'neath the sapphire cope
  Of deepening Heavens he hails a happier Day,
  And the spent Shadow mutely wanes away.

LUCETTE.

A snow-white brow, and tender eyes!
  A lip of rich carnation!
    A fairy's pace,
    And form of grace,
With the still glory on her face
  Of virgin meditation!

A snow-white mind! the tenderest heart
  That e'er bore Heaven reflected!
    A light, it seems,
    Of sacred dreams
(O radiant tide!) about her streams,
  The chrism of God's elected.

I greet her with a conscious thrill,
  — A strange and deep confusion, —
    As one who knows
    His crimes must close
Hope's portal to the Thought which rose,
  "Go! win her from seclusion!"

False am I, yet not false enough
 To link my base condition
  With her pure state,
  Forestalling Fate,
Who lurks with latent Joy in wait
 To crown her with fruition.

THE PICTURE OF A BEAUTIFUL DEATH.

A FRAGMENT.

They knew that she must leave them! day by day
Her spirit brightened through its veil of clay,
Till *that* seemed spirit also, — a fair Thing,
Poised for a moment on its luminous wing,
And soon, — oh! not to *die*, — but melt away
Into the perfect splendor: —

                              One calm morn,
— A July morn, — just as the sunshine kissed
From the dim summits of the broadening hills
The shadows of the twilight and the mist,
Amidst the faint-heard music of far rills,
With not a sight, nor tone, nor shade forlorn
In earth or heaven, — she rose from mystic dreams
To view once more the golden summer-gleams,
And say "farewell" to Nature; —

                                  Nature smiled,
And with majestic pity drew around
The failing footsteps of her favorite child
Her richest spells of beauty; — not a sound
But came with mellowed murmur, — not an air

THE PICTURE OF A BEAUTIFUL DEATH.

That touched her tranquil forehead, and dark hair,
But seemed a Seraph's whisper; the glad birds
Were full of carols, and the loving Sky
Bent, as it were, to clasp her; peaceful herds
Browsed on the distant slopes, and in the vale,
Still as a placid vision, the clear lake
Glassed the blue heaven's divine tranquillity, —
And every verdant shrub and blossoming brake
Glistened with dewy baptism.

* * * * * *

                              There she lay
As in the first mild sleep of infancy,
Her face upturned towards the quiet sky,
O'er which a white cloud floated silently,
— Most like an angel; — as the cloud crept on,
It threw a shadow struggling with a gleam
Right on her eyelids; slowly they unclosed
From the deep rapture of some glorious dream,
And the large eyes, clear with immortal life,
Shone out upon her mother; — then she sighed
One transient human sigh, — and so — she died.

And years have passed! — spring blooms, and wintry
    showers,
And gorgeous splendors of Autumnal eves
By turn have glorified, and chilled the spot
Her mortal form hath hallowed; — but the years

THE PICTURE OF A BEAUTIFUL DEATH.

Bring no reprieve to memory! — hast thou not,
O stricken Mother! ever in thy mind
A vision of thy darling 'mid the leaves
Of the young spring-vines dying? — pale as then,
But oh! so beautiful, so beautiful,
That murmuring to thyself, thou sayst again,
— As in a trance, — "daughter! the angels wait
To bear thee up!" —

                Alas! the Eden gate
Hath closed so long upon her, that ofttimes
A stress of rayless misery weighs thee down;
Thou hear'st no hymn supernal, — but the chimes
Of funeral bells, — the everlasting crown
Pales by the spectral whiteness of her tomb! —

There shalt thou mourn through all the coming
    years,
And there, when Faith is darkened, drop thy tears.
God help thee lady! 'twas the bitterest blow!
Yet other hearts than thine were stricken low,
And other hopes eclipsed, when she departed;
Well, let us lean on Patience! *we* have done
With earthly gauds; the day is waxing late,
The sunset falls, the shadows are unfurled
About the Future, and I see thee stand,
O Mother! with thy loved one, hand in hand,
Beneath the palm-trees in the Better Land!

SONG.

I.

O! your eyes are deep and tender,
  O! your charmèd voice is low,
But I've found your beauty's splendor
  All a mockery and a show;
Slighted heart and broken promise
  Follow wheresoe'er you go.

II.

All your words are fair and golden,
  All your actions false and wrong,
Not the noblest soul's beholden
  To your weak affections long;
Only true in — lover's fancy,
  Only constant in — his song.

LINES.

"THOUGH DOWERED WITH INSTINCTS KEEN AND HIGH."

> He weeps
> His youth, and its brave hopes, all dead and gone,
> In tears which burn. — PARACELSUS.

THOUGH dowered with instincts keen and high,
   With burning thoughts that wooed the light,
The scornful world hath passed him by,
   And left him lonelier than the Night;

Yes! cold and helpless; one by one,
   The stars of Faith have quenched their flame,
And, like a waning Polar sun,
   Declines the latest hope of Fame.

He longed to sing one noble song,
   To thrill, with passion's living breath,
The fools whose scorn had worked him wrong, —
   To baffle Fate, and conquer Death.

Dear God! dost thou endow with powers,
   Whose aspirations mock the bars

Of time and sense,— whose vision towers
   Irradiate 'mid thy sovereign stars,

Only to furnish some faint gleams
   Of loftier Beauty, quick withdrawn,
Leaving a frenzied hell of dreams,
   And wailings for the vanished Dawn?

The Oracles of Fancy mute,—
   Ambition's Priests dethroned and fled,
He wanders with a tuneless lute,
   Through dreary regions of the dead.

But from that place of bale uploom
   The Phantoms of unburied years,
The haunting Care, the Grief, the Gloom,
   The treacherous Hopes, the pale-eyed Fears,

That stormed his spirit's brave design,
   That clogged its wings,— betrayed its trust,—
Defaced its creed,— and dashed the wine,
   In Song's bright chalice to the dust.

Ah! Heaven! could He retrace his life
   From out this realm of doubt and dearth,
He would not court Thought's eagle strife,
   But clasp the Peace that clings to earth.

Above, the threatening thunders wait,
    And lightnings watch the souls that soar,
But lowly lives are safe from hate,
    And humblest aims, the wisest lore.

Yet — birds that breast the turbulent air,
    Are worthier than the things that creep, —
And nobler is a HIGH DESPAIR
    Than weak content — or sluggish sleep.

THE EVE OF THE BRIDAL.

AND *hath* it come, that strange, o'ermastering Hour,
When blushing Hope, and tender, tremulous Fears
Sway the full heart with a divided power,
Alternate sunshine and alternate tears?

Oh! for a spell to charm away thy care,
As I *could* charm were I but near thee now,
Chiding with lightsome laughter the despair, —
That girlish, coy despair that dims thy brow.

A fitful gloom that shades the flush of joy,
Like those transparent clouds in summer days,
That cast a silvery shadow, and destroy
The else unveiléd noon's too dazzling blaze.

Yet, from the far hills of this foreign shore,
I waft thee benedictions on the wind,
Hopes, that a peaceful Bliss forevermore
May rule the quiet Empire of thy mind.

And blessing thus, the darkening distance dies,
And in a grander than Agrippa's glass,
— The enamored Fancy, — a pale picture lies,
Brightening to shape and beauty ere it pass;

A room where sunset's glory, deep though dim,
Girds the rich chamber with luxurious grace,
Rounds the fair outline of each delicate limb,
And crowns with mellowed lustre thy sweet face.

In graceful folds thy loose robes, soft and rare,
Swell with the passionate heaving of thy breast,
O'er whose young loveliness the enchanted Air,
More golden seeming, seeks voluptuous rest.

Thy hand — in two brief hours no longer thine —
Gleams by a damask curtain, stirred with sighs,
And the full, starlike tears begin to shine
In the blue heaven of those bewildering eyes.

Tears for the girlhood, almost passed away,
Its innocent life, its wealth of tender lore,
Tears for the womanhood, whose opening day,
Glimmering, reveals the untried scenes before.

Not bitter tears! for him thou lov'st is true,
And all thy being trembles into flame,

A soft, delicious flame that thrills thee through,
Whene'er thy memory lingers on his name.

Even now I see thee turn thy timid head,
Luxuriant-tressed, towards a dim retreat,
Where twilight shadows veil thy bridal bed,
And purple Gloom, and amorous Silence meet.

A step! it is the approach of her, whose hands
— Dear hands — long to array thee for the rite,
Which draws around thy life the welcome bands
Of wedded joys and duties, born to-night.

She comes! and soon enrobed in fairest guise,
Fresh as a rose the summer winds have wooed,
Thou goest to pledge thy faith in low replies,
And leave for aye thy virgin solitude.

And Peace go with thee; wheresoe'er thou art,
Blest be all sinless passion, like to thine,
And Heaven's divinest Angels guard the heart,
The inviolate heart, where true Love builds a
    shrine.

"HERE, WHEN I HAVE LAID ASIDE."

Here, when I have laid aside
　The cumbrous load of life,
By this rivulet's languid tide,
　Far from mortal strife, —
Let them make my quiet grave
Where the emerald grasses wave
　Flushed with woodland flowers,
And the birds, as Twilight dies,
Pour their genial harmonies
　Like falls of silver showers.

The skies that circle round the place
　Are purer than elsewhere,
And a spirit of rare grace
　Sanctifies the air;
Richer tints at day-dawn lie
On the dew-lit meadows nigh,
　And the sunset's glory
Floods the ancient hazel wood,
As a Poet's purple mood
　Floods an ancient story.

Tranquil voices whisper, "rest" —
  Rising from still streams,
Floated to the waning West,
  With the calm of dreams;
And the breeze's murmurous call
Hath the faint, ethereal fall
  Of songs in childhood's sleep;
And all things do seem to be
Parts of some lone mystery,
  Which broodeth sad and deep.

MY FATHER.

My Father! in the mist-enshrouded Past,
  My boyish thoughts have wandered o'er and o'er
  To thy lone grave upon a distant shore,
The wanderer of the waters, still at last.

Never in boyhood have I blithely sprung
  To catch my father's voice, or climb his knee;
  He was a constant Pilgrim of the sea,
And died upon it when his boy was young.

He perished not in conflict nor in flame,
  No laurel garland rests upon his tomb;
  Wild were his days, and clouded was his doom,
Brief was his life, forgotten is his name.

Yet have I shrined his memory in my mind,
  Yet have I wrought his image on my soul —
  Though fancy-painted, a most perfect whole
Of sweet conceptions, deep, though dim-defined.

His careless bearing, and his manly face,
  His frank, bold eye, his tall and stalworth form

Fitted to breast the fight, the wreck, the storm;
The sailor's *nonchalance*, the soldier's grace.

In dreams, in dreams we've mingled, and a swell
  Of feeling mightier for the eye's eclipse,
  The music of a blest Apocalypse,
Hath murmured through my spirit, like a spell.

Ah, then! ofttimes a sadder scene will rise,
  A gallant vessel through the mist-bound day,
  Lifting her spectral spars above the bay,
Swayed gloomily against the glimmering skies.

O'er the dim billows thundering, peals a boom
  Of the deep gun that bursteth as a knell,
  When the brave tender to the brave farewell,—
And strong arms bear a comrade to the tomb.

*   *   *   *   *   *

The opened sod; a sorrowing band beside—
  One rattling roll of musketry, and then,
  A man no more among his fellow-men,
Darkness his chamber, and the Earth his bride,

My father sleeps in peace; perchance more blest
  Than some he left to mourn him, and to know
  The bitter blight of an enduring woe,
Longing (how oft!) with him to be at rest.

THE WILL, AND THE WING.

To have the will to soar, but not the wings, —
Eyes fixed forever on a starry height,
Whence stately shapes of grand imaginings
Flash down the splendors of imperial light,

And yet to lack the charm that makes them ours,
The obedient vassals of that conquering spell,
Whose omnipresent and ethereal powers
Encircle Heaven, nor fear to enter Hell;

This is the doom of Tantalus — the thirst
For beauty's balmy fount, to quench the fires
Of the wild passion that our souls have nurst
In hopeless promptings, — unfulfilled desires.

Yet would I rather in the outward state
Of Song's immortal Palace lay me down,
A beggar basking by that golden gate,
Than bend beneath the haughtiest Empire's crown.

For sometimes, through the bars, my trancéd eyes
Have caught the vision of a life divine,
And seen a far, mysterious rapture rise
Beyond the veil that guards the inmost shrine.

THE PESTILENCE.

WRITTEN DURING THE PREVALENCE OF THE YELLOW FEVER IN CHARLESTON, S. C., IN THE SUMMER OF 1858.

How long, O Lord! shall Desolation hold
Stern empire over us, and wasteful Death
Darken the sunshine, and the life of hope?
Fierce Harvester! Oh! whither stretch the bounds
Of thy permitted vengeance? hast thou not
In thy cold granary heaped the human grain
Sheaf upon sheaf? — is not the harvest ended,
Or nigh its end? — most precious household bonds
Of wifehood, childhood, brotherhood, all ties
Which twine with tenderest thrill around our hearts,
— And parted leave them broken, — thy swift scythe
Hath severed; barren hast thou left the field
Thou found'st so rich in fruitage; spare the rest,
The few, sad, shivering stalks that droop i' th' wind
Mourning their prostrate brethren.

THE PESTILENCE.

                              God of might!
How fearful art thou when in cloud and fire,
Thou send'st thy pitiless messengers to smite
The doomèd nations! then this beautiful earth,
Changed to a pestilent charnel, opes her womb
Unutterably loathsome, where DECAY
Sits mocking at our motley human pomps,
Our pride, and even the sacred passionate grief
Wherewith we mourn its victims; — hollow masks
Hiding a dark Reality, seem all
Man's shows, conventions, forms, howe'er august.
Death pricks them with his keen Ithurial lance,
And lo! from out their gilded impotence crawls
"THE CONQUEROR WORM!"
                    —— Hard it is for Faith
Amidst these mortal vapors, — these foul damps
Corrupt, and earthy, to lift up her wings
Dank with sepulchral dew, and win the light
Which still shines calm above them; her fair face,
Furrowed with scathing tears, hath lost its clear
Angelic courage, and her faltering voice, —
Faint as the tremulous accents of fourscore, —
Can only whisper feebly, "WATCH, AND PRAY!"

RETROSPECTION AND ASPIRATION.

The fiery glow of sunset pales,
And soft adown the deepening vales
The tranquil shadows steal apace;
The winds repose, the waters keep
The stillness of unbroken sleep,
And all the unmeasured realm of space
Between us, and the stars that rise
To crown those rich imperial skies,
Majestic Silence holds in thrall:
Only — the quiet dews that fall
In stealthy dripping from the eaves,
Or some lone bird among the leaves,
Touched by a transient dream of flight,
Stir to the faintest thrill of sound,
The mystery of the Calm profound.

The peace of Heaven is in my heart!
And if that God would grant me grace,
I could lie down in this sweet place,
Breathe *Nunc Dimittis!* — and depart!

I stand forlorn, where last the light
Of her mild beauty blessed my sight; —
Oh! she, so generous in her trust,
So queenly in her maiden pride, —
(The pride of perfect womanhood
That crowneth with its regal sweetness
All meaner creatures' incompleteness,)
Was near to blend the brightening charm
Of her entrancing human eyes
With Nature's beauty, and make warm
With whisperings of a human love —
Born of all tender sympathies —
The else cold pulses of the air.

Soul! thou alone art altered here!
Around me sways the orange grove,
The self-same grove that heard our vows,
And waved its glad melodious boughs,
Setting to music all she said,
And showering on her gracious head
White flowers, as if to crown a bride:

Just on an eve like this, she died —
So still and fair — I saw her die,
Bound by a spell of misery
Too bitter for the balm of sighs, —
That froze the tears within mine eyes,

The currents of my brain and blood;
The while, as statue-wan, I stood
As one who in the lonely trance
Of some unearthly dark Romance,
Hath heard a ghostly voice of doom
Wailing above an open tomb.

Love! lift me to thy radiant clime, —
I sicken on the waste of Time,
And burn to breathe a subtler breath
Than that which haunts these realms of death;
For round about me float and stir
Foul vapors from the sepulchre,
Rising, — a monstrous gloom, — to blight
The glory of the inner sight —
Shrouding phantasmal shapes of ill, —
But *thou*, the same sweet Angel still,
Thou canst not leave me thus forlorn,
And exiled from the gates of Morn!

Within my soul a vision glows,
A vision of the peace to be,
The undivined serenity,
In whose clear depths the angels dwell:
Through many a fiery-circled Hell
Of self-inflicted woe and pain,
Through many lives — (for still I hold

That not in vain above us rolled,
The mighty Planets whirl in space, —
Each is the destined dwelling-place
Of souls, fresh-winged in every star, —)
We struggle toward the holy Height,
The consummation infinite,
Whereto the groaning Ages tend:

A prescient Voice foretells the End
O Voice that fallest faint and far,
Sound on through all our dreary night;

" From height to height the soul aspires,
Reluming its mysterious fires
Through the vast worlds which gird the way
Up to the immemorial Day
Of primal Immortality!"

Ah! that I then may meet with thee
In that serene Eternity!
May feel that human love *can* shine
Unwavering 'midst the Love Divine,
May rise on Rapture's eagle wing,
And hear the spheral music ring,
And that great Song the Seraphs sing
Peal round the Godhead's Mystery, —
And mark, where grosser systems trace

Their orbits in the outcast space,
Earth with its transient agonies
Sink from the height of those calm skies
Down to a gulf so dim and low,
They flicker to a fire-fly glow,
Myths of a million years ago!

"THE LAUGHING HOURS BEFORE HER FEET."

The laughing Hours before her feet
  Are scattering Spring-time roses,
And the voices in her soul are sweet
  As music's mellowed closes;
All hopes and passions heavenly-born,
  In her have met together,
And Joy diffuses round her morn
  A mist of golden weather.

As o'er her cheek of delicate dyes
  The blooms of childhood hover,
So do the tranced and sinless eyes
  All childhood's heart discover.
Full of a dreamy happiness,
  With rainbow fancies laden,
Whose arch of promise glows to bless
  Her spirit's beauteous Aidenn.

She is a being born to raise
  Those undefiled emotions
That link us with our sunniest days
  And most sincere devotions.

In her we see renewed and bright,
  That phase of earthly story,
Which glimmers in the morning light
  Of God's exceeding glory.

Why in a life of mortal cares
  Appear these heavenly faces?
Why on the verge of darkened years
  These Amaranthine graces?
Oh! 'tis to cheer the soul that faints
  With true and blest Evangels,
To prove if heaven is rich with Saints,
  That earth may have her Angels.

Enough! 'tis not for *me* to pray
  That on her life's sweet river
The calmness of a virgin day
  May rest, and rest forever;
I know a guardian Genius stands
  Beside those waters lowly,
And labors with immortal hands
  To keep them pure, and holy.

SONNET.

VAINLY a hostile world may strive to tame
The Poet's soul through Love, and Grief made strong;
Unfettered still, he soars to heights of Song,
Whence his clear genius sheds a starlike flame.
Deaf to the captious sneer, the ignorant blame,
He sings of heavenly RIGHT, and mortal WRONG,
Of faith and sufferance, that by birth belong
To noble spirits,— and that final fame
Which crowns their shining brows with Amaranth bloom:
No shallow discontent, with fretful moan,
Mars his brave utterance,— no unmanly gloom
Shadows *his* heart wherein Hope reigns alone;
For rebel Doubts his nature hath no room,
Scorning to be thus basely overthrown!

SONNET.

Moments there are when most familiar things
Seem strangers to us; when 'round heart and head
The mists of unreality are spread,
From which our keenest searching, baffled, brings
Unformed conceptions, vague imaginings,
Tinged with the doubtful hues of a half-truth;
Chiefly in age, or in our dreaming youth
This phase of contemplation sternly wrings
Our bosoms with the thought, — "the soul is blind!"
Unfathomed meanings, beauty most divine,
Lie round about us, — but we cannot see;
In sky and forest burns a spirit's sign
Unrecognized, and in the whispering wind
Breathes a low undertone of mystery!

DRAMATIC SKETCHES.

ANTONIO MELIDORI.

[AMONG the heroes of the modern Greek Revolution, none, perhaps, were so distinguished for acts of individual daring, and a spirit of romantic and chivalrous adventure, as the Captain Antonio Melidori, a native of Candia. He waged against the Turks a partisan conflict, which was often eminently successful. His own deeds of strength, and reckless hardihood, made him terrible to the foe, who were persuaded finally to look upon him as one whose life was "charmed."

It did not prove so, however, as he fell a victim to the rage and jealousy of some of his own company. Having been invited by the malcontents to a feast, Rousso, (the chief of the conspirators, whom Antonio appears to have rivalled successfully both in love and war,) whilst in the very act of embracing the patriot, plunged a dagger into his bosom.

There is a tradition that Antonio loved a beautiful maiden, PHILÓTA, whom in the stirring and anxious scenes of the Revolution he was ultimately led to neglect, if not to forsake. A writer in "Chambers's Journal" has from this episode in the private career of the Greek partisan taken the *matériel* for a touching and graphic narrative, which has been closely, often literally followed in the composition of the ensuing "sketch."

The author had intended, at one time, to compose a tragedy of the usual length upon this subject, but he has never been able to proceed beyond a few Scenes, which, however, appear to him to possess a certain unity of their own. They are now published partly with the hope of calling the attention of some more practised dramatic writer, (the brilliant author of " Anne Boleyn " and " Calaynos " for example), — to a theme eminently picturesque and suggestive.]

SCENE I.

[A place not far from the summit of Mount Psiloriti, in the Isle of Candia. PHILÓTA discovered with a basket of grapes upon her head; she looks eagerly upward. Time, a little before sunset.]

PHILÓTA.

Why comes he not? here on this emerald sward,
Close to the cool shade of these ancient rocks,
We have met, and fondly communed in the sunset
Eve after eve, since first he said, "I love thee!" —
Never, Antonio, hast thou been ere now
A loiterer! wherefore should my heart beat fast,
And my breath thicken, and the dew of fear
Stand chill upon my forehead? is't an omen?

[*At this moment* ANTONIO *is seen bounding quickly down the mountain; he reaches* PHILÓTA, *and embraces her.*]

ANTONIO.

Thou hast waited long, Philóta, hast thou not?

PHILÓTA.

'Tis true, Antonio! but thou know'st an hour,
Nay, a bare minute, drags the weariest length
When thou art from me!

ANTONIO.

Thanks, dearest, and — forgive me,
I did but dream upon the hill-top yonder,
And dreaming thus — forgot thee —

PHILÓTA.

Forgot me! —

ANTONIO.

Nay, nay, I meant not *that!* thy face, thy smiles,
Thy deep devotion, — in my heart of hearts
I keep *them* shrined forever, — but my thoughts
Turned truant, — who can hold his thoughts, Philóta,
In a leash always? — prithee **reascend**
The mountain with me, I would show the place
Which tempted my weak thoughts to wander thus.

[*They reach the most elevated portion of the mountain, whence a wide circuit of land and sea becomes visible.*]

PHILÓTA.

How beautiful! how glorious! see, my Love,
There's not a cloud, or shadow of cloud in Heaven!

Even here, the winds breathe faintly, and afar
O'er the broad circuit of the watery calm,
Peace broods upon the Ocean, rules the Air,
And up the sunset's dazzling pathway walks
Like a Saint entering Paradise.

       'Twere sweet,
How sweet, Antonio, amid scenes like these,
To live and love forever!

    ANTONIO, [*absently.*]

      Dost thou think so?
Aye! — well — perhaps ——

    PHILÓTA.

     He heeds me not, his eye
Is cold and stern — what troubles thee, Antonio?

    ANTONIO.

Trouble! I am not troubled.

    PHILÓTA.

      But thou art,
I *know* thou art; would'st thou deceive Philóta?

    ANTONIO.

Now by the Saints, not so; dismiss the fear
Which, like a tremulous shadow, breaks the calm

Of those soft eyes! [*after a pause*]
                      The matter, in brief, is this:
Tracking our mountain paths at early dawn,
Rousso — thou knowest him — hailed me from the
    rocks,
With words that sounded like the battle trumpets.
"It comes!" he cried, "the war-cloud rolls this way;
We too shall hear its thunders"——

PHILÓTA.
                      Aye! and feel
Its bolts perchance, — there's lightning in such clouds!

ANTONIO.
What if there be! who would not brave them all,—
All, for a cause like ours? Believe me, Love,
We stand upon the brink of troublous times!
All shall be changed here: men,— brave Grecian
    men, —
The blood of heroes in them, — cannot pause,
Storing the honey, trampling down the olive,
Or humbly following the tame herdsman's trade,
Whilst Freedom calls to conflict.
                      Look, Philóta!
Dost mark yon lurid flash across the bay?
Our soldiers test their cannon! hark, below,
The drums of Affendouli — how they ring!

Already thousands of bold Mountaineers
Have formed beneath his banners; dost thou hear
    me?

PHILÓTA.

And would'st *thou* wish to join them? Ah! I see,
I see it all!—a trouble on thy brow,
Borne upward from the restless gloom within,
Hath clouded o'er thy peace. I,—a frail girl,
And gifted only with the wealth of *love*,—
How can *I* satisfy the burning need
Of a strong man's ambition? Yes, 'tis so,
'Tis even so!—love is the woman's heaven,
Her hope, her God, her life-blood! yet to *man*,
What is it but a pastime?

ANTONIO.

                Speak not thus,
Oh, speak not thus, Philóta! I have loved
Thee, only thee,—so help me, Virgin Mother!
But comrades from whose lips a taunt is bitter,
Have dared to hint——

PHILÓTA.

        What!

ANTONIO.

              That I chose to stay,

Delving, like some base Slave, our barren soil,
When not a Sphakiote that can carry arms
Has failed to seize them. Liars! foul-mouthed liars,
I would have *proved* the falsehood were it not ——

Philóta.

For *me* — Philóta! — well! I love thee dearly,
Deeply, — God knows, — but I would have this love
To crown thee as a garland, — not as a chain
To bind and fetter — thou art free, Antonio! —

Antonio.

But hast thou thought of all which follows this?
Thou shalt be left alone, no bridal feast
Can cheer the olive harvest!

Philóta.

     I *have* thought,
And am determined; — thou art free, Antonio! —

Antonio.

Oh, thanks, thanks, thanks! — lift up thy hopes,
 Philóta,
Up to the height of mine! our cause is just,
And a just Fate shall guard it; wheresoe'er
Free thought finds utterance, and the patriot-soul
Thrills at the deeds of heroes, — we may look

For a " God speed ! " The prayers of noble men,
The tears of women, — the whole world's applause
Do wait upon us ! . . .
     Methinks I see the end,
A free, grand Commonwealth of Grecian States,
Built upon chartered rights, — each sealed with
 blood !

PHILÓTA.

Enough ! enough ! Antonio, thou shalt go ! —
Greece is thy mistress now.

SCENE II.

[The cottage of PHILÓTA, at the foot of Mount Psiloriti. PHILÓTA discovered at the window, looking out upon the night, which is bleak and stormy.]

PHILÓTA.

Hark ! how those lusty Trumpeters, the Winds,
Urge on the black battalions of the clouds ;
And see ! the swollen rivulets rushing down
The sides of Psiloriti ! — yesterday,
'Neath the clear calm of the serenest Morn
Earth ever stole from Paradise, they swept
— Bright curves of laughing silver in the sunshine,
But now, — an overmastering rush of floods, —

They thunder to the Heavens, that answer back
From the wild depths of gloom, — an awful
   tempest!

[*Enter* ANTONIO *hastily.*]

ANTONIO.

Where is the priest, Philóta? where is Andreas?
Was he not here to night?—

PHILÓTA.

Aye! but he left some half hour since;

ANTONIO.

                    What say you?
Oh, the poor father!—then 'twas *him* I saw
Pent 'twixt the mountain torrents; he is lost!
The good old man!—and yet, not so, not so!
Give me yon oaken staff,— and, hold!—a flask
Of the best vintage;— I'll be back anon,
And the dear father with me:—

[*Exit* ANTONIO. PHILÓTA *kneels before an image of the Virgin, and prays for the safety of her lover. After the lapse of some minutes, enter* ROUSSO *stealthily, wrapped in a cloak, which partly conceals his features.*]

ROUSSO, [*aside.*]

                    Faith! a pretty picture!

Now, were I what fools call poetical,
I'd worship *her*, whilst *she* adores the Saint,—
A lovelier Saint herself, and nearer truly
To the just standard of Divinity,
Than yonder painted image; there's the curve,
The old Greek curve, in the voluptuous swell
Of those full lips; the passion in her eyes
Is shadowed off to melancholy meaning,
Only to waken to meridian life,
When a like passion touches it to flame:

PHILÓTA, [*praying.*]

Oh, merciful Mother! save him,— save Antonio!

ROUSSO, [*aside.*]

Oh, potent Devil! claim him,— claim Antonio!
What! shall this malapert boy dispute *my* love?

[PHILÓTA, *rising, discovers* ROUSSO, *towards whom (mistaking him for* ANTONIO*) she rushes, as if about to cast herself into his arms, but discovering her error she shrinks back.*]

PHILÓTA.

You here!

ROUSSO, [*advancing.*]

I crave protection, shelter,— may I stay?

PHILÓTA.

At a safe distance, Sir!

ROUSSO.

Why, what means this?
I looked for kindlier welcome!

PHILÓTA.

Wherefore, Rousso?
What thou hast asked, I grant, — protection, shelter;
Durst thou claim more than these?

ROUSSO.

I' faith thy temper is most strange and wayward!
Because, — some months agone, not quite myself,
I ventured at the harvest of the Olive,
Upon one innocent liberty ——

PHILÓTA.

No *liberty*,
With *me* at least, bold man! is rated thus!

ROUSSO.

I do repeat, that I was not myself;
Blame the hot wine of Cyprus; spare your
    slave! [*kneeling.*]

Philóta.

A slave indeed! —

Rousso.

But one who stoops to conquer, fair Philóta;
If I *have* knelt, 'tis only that I may
Rise thus, and clasp thee! Hold, no foolish cries,
No weak, vain strugglings! Think'st thou that the storm
Pealing adown the mountain's rugged steeps,
Can bear these feeble wailings to thy friends? —
Come, come, Philóta! — if thou could'st believe it,
I am the very worthiest of thy vassals; —
List for an instant, while I paint the beauty
Of a far Eden waiting for the light,
The sundawn of thine eyes: —

—— Amid the waves
Of the Ægean, bosomed in the calm
Of ever-during summer, sleeps an Isle
Whereon the Ocean ripples into music, —
Through whose luxuriant wilderness of blooms,
The soft winds sigh their breath away in dreams,
Where — [the deuce take me! I forget my part] —
Where — where — where — i' sooth, a place
To live, to love, to die in, and revisit
From the sad vale of shadows, with a touch
Of mortal fondness, overmastering death;
Wilt thou go thither with me? Nay, thou must!

[*As* Rousso *attempts to carry* Philóta *from the apartment, she recovers, and by a sudden effort releases herself from his arms.*]

Rousso.

    Pardon, Philóta! 'tis my eager *love*
Which thus hath urged me on; thou tremblest!—
 what?
I would not make thee fear me;—

Philóta.

     Fear! fear!
If my cheek pales, it is not cowardice
That plays the tyrant to the exiled blood;
If my frame trembles, there are other moods
Than that thou speak'st of, to unstring its firmness;
Thy presence brings no *terrors;* dost thou talk
Of *fear* to a Greek woman?—

Rousso.

    No! no! not fear, but *love!*

Philóta.

      Man! man, I pray thee
Blaspheme not thus!—what canst *thou* know of love?
'Tis true thou speak'st it boldly; from thy lips
The word falls with a rounded fullness off,—
And yet, believe me, thou hast used a phrase,

(A sacred phrase, and wretchedly profaned,) —
Which, were thy years thrice lengthened out beyond
The general limit of our mortal lives,
And thou be made to pass through all extremes
Of multiform experience, it could never
Enter thy sordid soul to comprehend! —

Rousso.

Bravely delivered! by my soul, I think
We *both* make good declaimers! Where did'st learn
That pretty speech, Philóta?

Philóta.

                    Wilt thou leave me?

Rousso.

Pshaw! thou art less than courteous! Leave thee! no!
I will not leave thee! Hark ye, my proud damsel,
I am not one with whom 'tis safe to trifle, —
Thou knowest, or *shalt* know this; so, mark my words, —
Long have I wooed thee fairly, would have won thee,
Yea, and endowed thee with both wealth and station; —

Twice hast thou heard my proffer, twice with loathing
Spurned it, and me;—I shall not woo thee thrice
With honeyed words; no, 'tis the strong arm now.
I am prepared for all,—come on!

[*He seizes* PHILÓTA *a second time, but enter on the instant* ANTONIO, *with the Monk* ANDREAS *leaning upon him.*]

PHILÓTA, [*faintly.*]

Saved! saved!

ANTONIO.

Ha, Rousso, I have heard it whispered oft
Amongst thy watchful brethren in this isle,
That underneath that smooth and flattering front
There lurked a mine of blackest villany!
I did deny it once; what shall I say
When next the public voice decries you Sir?

ROUSSO.

A jest!—I do assure you but a jest!
This cloak, which in your self-devoted flight
To rescue the dear father, Andreas,—
[How glad I am to see his Saintship safe,]
You dropped some furlongs from the mountain's base,
I cast, in sportive fashion, on my person,—
And deeming that Philóta would rejoice
To hear that thou had'st so far braved the force

O' th' treacherous elements, — I called upon her;
She did me the vast honor to confound
Your humble servant with Antonio, —
And 'ere I was aware, sprang to my arms,
With such a blinded ecstacy of rapture,
That I had wellnigh sunk into the Earth,
From the mere stress of native modesty!
A jest, — a jest, — and nothing but — a jest.

ANTONIO.

Such jesting may be dangerous, — beware!

SCENE III.

[*A year is supposed to have elapsed. The town of Sphakia after nightfall. Enter confusedly a band of Sphakiote soldiers, with Rousso amongst them. The streets are crowded with women, many of whom are heard lamenting the death of* ANTONIO MELIDORI.]

Rousso, [in a disguised voice.]

Why will ye clamor thus, ye foolish jades?
Your handsome favorite, your renowned commander,
Is no more dead than I am!

A WOMAN.

Say'st thou so?
Where then is Melidori?

Rousso, [*still disguising his voice.*]

       Would'st thou learn?
Women of Sphakia, your immaculate Captain, —
He for whose welfare, upon bended knees,
Ye nightly pray to Heaven, — whose name your infants
Lisp in their very slumbers, — hath betrayed us! —
Hold! — hear me out! — I am no dubious witness;
Thrice, whilst the battle raged along our front,
I saw the Traitor creeping like a dog
Between the Turkish outposts! —

[ANTONIO *appears in the rear, with a child in his arms.*]

ANTONIO.

      It is false! —
Here is your leader, Sphakiotes; what base slanderer
Dares to pronounce me Traitor? I but paused
To save this weeping innocent, whose mother
Fell by some coward's sword!

ROUSSO.

     Ha, Sphakiotes, see,
The noble Melidori waxes tender, —
Soft as a woman! — *he* must love the Moslem,
Who fosters thus their offspring! — by the Saints
A lusty brat! he'll thrive, good friends, believe me,
And grow betimes, — to cut *our* infant's throats!

ANTONIO.

Let him who speaks stand forth; I would confront
My bold accuser. What! he clings to the dark!—
Fit place for lies, and liars!

                              Friends, I scorn
To parley with this viper; there's a way,
One only way, to deal with reptiles,— crush them,—
Thus,— thus,— and thus,—
When they have crawled too near us;
      [*Stamping violently upon the earth.*]
Till then, why let the ugly beasts hiss on,
And spit their harmless venom:—
      [*Turning to the women.*]

                              Mothers, wives,
Maidens of Sphakia, are there none amongst ye
Ready to take this poor unfortunate?
Just for *my* sake, fair countrywomen, list,
List to the blessèd word:— " The merciful
Shall obtain mercy!"—

ROUSSO.

                         Heed him not, I say,
But seize the infidel whelp, and let him rock
On a steel bayonet! What! have we repelled
The invading foe, exterminated wholly
His forces, and his empire, that we dare
Cherish his cubs among us?—and for what?

"Just for *his* sake, fair countrywomen, — his,
And mercy's!" Who showed mercy to *our* children,
When the Turk ravaged Scio? The young devil, —
Hear how he shrieks! ho! send him down to
　　Hell!
Down to his Father! he's a grateful Spirit,
And thankful for small favors!

[*The crowd begin to murmur, and move threateningly towards* ANTONIO.]

ANTONIO.

　　　　　　　　Shame upon you!
Though the poor boy were fifty times a Moslem,
I'll rear him as my own; he shall not perish;
Perchance, who knows, when I have died for
　　you, —
For you, and Grecian liberty, this babe,
Reared as a Greek, may yet avenge my death,
As none of *you*, false brethren, dare avenge it!
Once more I say, — Mothers, wives, maids of
　　Sphakia,
Is there not one amongst ye to whose tendance
I may commit this trembling castaway? —

PHILÓTA, [*veiled.*]

Give *me* the child, — I'll nurture him with love,
And gentlest usage.

ANTONIO, [*starting.*]

     Heavens! what voice is that?
You here Philóta? I had hoped you dwelt
Safely within the close heart of the mountains!

PHILÓTA.

The mountains are not safe.

ANTONIO.

      Why then did'st thou
Keep such strict silence? Answer me, Philóta,
How hast thou lived, — this peasant's dress——

PHILÓTA.

       Is fittest
For me, Antonio, — by my handiwork,
And daily labor, I do earn my bread, —
For was it meet an unknown peasant girl
Should claim, as her betrothed, great Melidori,
Captain of Sphakia?

ANTONIO.

     O, thou generous heart!
But stay, — the rabble must not catch our words;
Take thou the babe, — under the city-walls,
I'll meet thee in the gloaming.

SCENE IV.

[A place under the city walls,—time, an hour after sunset.]

ANTONIO, [*embracing* PHILÓTA *[constrainedly.]*]

How kind thou art!

PHILÓTA.

I but obeyed your mandate!

ANTONIO.

Nay, why so cold? my troth is thine Philóta,—
Dost thou remember?

PHILÓTA.

Would'st thou have me do so?
Methought *that* dream was over,—by *thy* wish.

ANTONIO.

By heaven! I never said so!

PHILÓTA.

Yet thy heart,
Thy heart, Antonio, spoke the keen desire,
Although thy lips kept silence;—I have learned
To read thy spirit like an open book,

And cannot be deceived; — all's changed with us;
Never again, as in the time that's past,
Shall we, hand linked in hand, explore the vales,
Or walk the shining hill-tops; — thou hast risen
Far, far above my level; — a great man,
Among the *greatest*, — thou wert mad t' espouse
A humble girl like me; — I ask it not; —
My love but burdens thy aspiring hopes,
So, I beseech thee, dwell no more upon it:
Antonio, for thy welfare I would give
My soul's life; shall I then refuse to yield
A personal joy, that thou may'st win, and wed
The immortal virgin — Glory? Dream it not! —
Oh! dream it not!

ANTONIO.

Now, gracious God forgive me!
It were presumption, should I kiss thy feet,
Thou pure, unselfish woman! — yet thy words
Are true, too true, — and I dare not gainsay them.
One thing believe, Philóta, I am wretched,
Yes, far more so than thou art:

[*After a pause.*]

— Did'st thou know
The terrible life I lead in this dread warfare,
Through what an atmosphere of blood and carnage
It is my doom to move, as through the air

Of some plague-stricken city, thick with curses,—
Did'st know the numberless dangers, that like de-
    mons,
(Many unseen,— and therefore doubly fearful,)
Which hover 'round the soldier, hour by hour
O'ershadowing life with the black gloom of death;
Did'st know the coarse companions, the rude manners
Of vile extortioners, bent alone on prey,
And personal profit,— and the thousand evils
Gendered of strife, and strife's unhallowed passions,—
O! thou would'st shrink from following such base
    courses,
Even as an Angel from the brink of Hell!

Philóta.

Thou wrong'st my love, and hast deceived thyself!
Where'er *thou* art, to me that place is Heaven;
Antonio!— God alone,— God, and my soul
Know what I might, and would have been to thee!—
I would have shared thy fortunes, joined my fate
For weal or woe, for honor or disgrace,
For life or death to thine;— have tracked thy steps,
(If need it were,) through seas of blood and
    carnage,—
Strengthened thy weakness, buoyed thy sinking
    hopes,
Nor, at the worst, have shed one woman's tear

To shake thy manhood! Had Heaven blessed thy cause,
I would have striven to make my spirit worthy
To mount with thee; so, when the orbéd glory
Shone like the fire of sunrise round thy brow,
No man dare say that with *that* lustre mingled
One blush of shame for Melidori's wife!—
This might have been, and this shall never be!
   [*Wildly.*]
I' th' name of mercy, by thy mother's soul,
And the dear past, I pray thee leave me now,
While still thou lov'st me, (dost thou not) a little?

ANTONIO.

And thou — and *thou* Philóta?——

PHILÓTA.

      I shall dwell
In peace; [*aside*] aye! broken hearts *are* peaceful!—

ANTONIO.

     But where?——

PHILÓTA.

What matter *where*, so that I live in peace?
Grieve not Antonio! in my humble station
One thought shall bring content;—" he was not false,"
No mortal maiden stole Antonio's heart!

ANTONIO.

      Blesséd words!
'Tis true I love but thee!—

PHILÓTA.

      Then do not sorrow!—
Love, I forgive thee!—thou hast wronged me not!
And for the child—ah!—I shall dream it thine,
Tend it as thine,—and when the years have
  ripened
That infant soul, 'tis mine to lead to virtue,
I'll teach the boy how noble was the act
Whereby Antonio saved him;—I'll be happy
Oh, trust me, Love! so very, *very* happy!——

ANTONIO.

Then be it so, Philóta! I would bless thee,
But am not worthy;—still, thou shalt be blessed.

PHILÓTA.

And thou, too, if the Virgin hear my prayers;
And now, that we are friends, *but* friends, though
  firm ones,
Beseech thee, list my tidings! There's a foe,
A deadly, treacherous foe in thine own camp,
And one who vows thy ruin; it is Rousso;
Thou knowest how first his envious, bitter temper

Was stung to hatred; since that time, thy will
Hath often clashed with his; besides, thy fame
In these fierce wars hath far o'ertopped *his* credit;
So he has sworn thy death; — the voice was his,
That goaded on thy soldiers to rebellion;
And, — as I threaded my uncertain pathway,
A short hour since, through the dark streets of
    Sphakia,
I heard thy name in whispers; — two dim forms,
[Men, as I knew by their hoarse tones,] conferred
With hurried, stealthy gestures, and one sentence
Startled me like a knell; — " His tomb is open,"
A deep voice said, — " Antonio's tomb is open!"
Oh, then, beware! — as lowly as thou deem'st me,
I'll watch above thy safety, — the soft dove
May warn the eagle of the midnight spoiler! —

ANTONIO.

And thy own life and safety ——

PHILÓTA.

                        I am here
To spend them both for thee! — but hark, thy name
Is shouted by thy comrades in the valley, —
The hour has come that parts us; — fare thee well!
    [*She gives him her hand.*]

ANTONIO.

'Twas not our wont to part in this cold fashion;
Come, one more kiss Philóta! let me feel
We *were* indeed betrothed; — one last, last kiss!

[*They embrace and part.*]

SCENE V.

[An apartment in the house of AFFENDOULI, the Governor-General of Candia. Enter ANTONIO, and AFFENDOULI, conversing.]

AFFENDOULI.

These private bickerings are the fruitful cause
Of all disgrace, and failure; — let us end them!

ANTONIO.

Most willingly! *I* have no feud with any,
Saving *one* quarrel, *forced* upon me, Chief! —

AFFENDOULI.

True, true! but even now a Courier waits,
Charged with a special message of good will,
From Rousso, and his brother, Anagnosti; —
They say, — "We plead for peace! — all personal hate
Henceforth be quelled between us; — we would join
Our troop to Melidori's, and our banners
Wave side by side with *his*." Accept their proffer!

ANTONIO.

I will!

AFFENDOULI.

To show thou art sincere, fail not to test
Their hospitality; —

ANTONIO.

As how? —

AFFENDOULI.

They give
A solemn feast of Unity and Friendship,
To which *thou* art invited. Go, I charge thee!

ANTONIO.

Trust me, I shall be there, — what day's appointed
Whereon to hold this festival of love?

AFFENDOULI.

This very day; thou knowest the camp of Rousso?

ANTONIO.

Ay! I'll be there anon! —

[*Exit* ANTONIO. *Enter, after a brief interval*, PHILÓTA, *with a hurried and anxious mien.*]

PHILÓTA.

Oh, pardon, pardon! Most gracious Governor! but I come to seek Ant—— Ant——, that is, the Captain Melidori, With tidings of grave import.

AFFENDOULI.

Ha! Thou luckless messenger! he has departed,— Gone——

PHILÓTA, [*wildly*.]

Where, where?—

AFFENDOULI.

To feast with Rousso.

PHILÓTA, [*rushing out*.]

Then is he lost! O merciful God, protect us!

SCENE VI.

[An open space in a wood,—tables arranged for a banquet,—Rousso, Anagnosti, Antonio Melidori, and their followers, discovered feasting.]

ANAGNOSTI.

A soldier's life forever! free to pass

In feast or fray! how glorious this wild banquet
Compared to those dull, formal feasts of old,
Held at the Olive harvest! Speak, Antonio,
Give us thy thought upon it; what! art silent?

Rousso.

Urge him no more; perchance Antonio pines
For the sweet quiet of that mountain life,
Which thou hast called so dull; its days of
    dream,
Its nights of warm voluptuous dalliance!

Antonio.

No, no, by Heaven! those times are dead to me;
They had their pleasures, but not one to match
The keen delights of glory,— the true honor
Which follows patriot service;—

Rousso.

                      Gallant words,
Brave, and high-sounding; but for me and mine,—
We do not fight for shadows!

Antonio, [*coldly.*]

                          I'm at fault,
Not clearly comprehending, Sir, your meaning.

Rousso.

Oh! thou dost well to speak of glory, honors,—
We know what rich rewards await thee, Chief,
When the war's ended;—spoils, and wealth and
    beauty!
But yestermorn, I saw thy winsome lady,
The bride to be,—old Affendouli's daughter.
Nay, shrink not man,—she is a lovely maid,
Fair as her father's generous;—what an eye!
Half arch, half languishing; and what a breast!
That heaves as 'twould burst outward to the day.
And strike men mad with its white panting pas-
    sion!
No lovelier woman lives, unless—unless—
It be that poor young thing who doted on thee,
Before the war,—what was her name?—Philóta?

Antonio.

Thy thoughts run on fair damsels; let us talk
Like soldiers, not like brain-sick boys in love.

Rousso.

With all my heart; only, one pledge to thee,
And Affendouli's daughter!—

Antonio.

    I have borne

This jesting with the patience of a Saint,
But now 'tis stretched to licence. Prithee cease!

Rousso.

God, how he winces!—if Philóta—

Antonio.

        Villain!
Utter that sacred name again——

Rousso, [*rising suddenly and drawing his dagger.*]

        Oh, ho!
Wilt fight, wilt fight!—I'm ready for thee; come.

Antonio, [*aside.*]

(He shall not trap me thus.) Thou art my host;—
'Twere shame, yea bitter shame this brawl should end
In blows and bloodshed!—when the time befits,—

   [*To* Rousso.]

Doubt not that I shall call thee to account
For this day's work;—meanwhile I leave a board
Where clownish insult poisons all your cups!

[*As he is about to depart,* Anagnosti *approaches, with an air of conciliation.*]

Anagnosti.

Well spoken, noble Captain, thou wert wronged;

But Rousso is so hasty! He repents;—
Let not this solemn feast of Unity
Break up in discord.

Rousso.

     No, no, no, Antonio!—
I *do* repent! Prithee embrace me, friend,
In sign of reconcilement.

[Rousso *approaches* Melidori *with an unsteady step; while in the act of embracing, he stabs him in the side.* Philóta *rushes upon the scene, with a cry of agony, and throws herself beside* Antonio, *whose head she supports.*]

Philóta.

Too late! O God, too late! He faints, he dies!
Why stare ye thus upon us, cruel men?
Wine, wine,—another cup, how slow ye move!
My scarf is drenched with blood,—ye pitiless fools!
Will not a creature loan me wherewithal
To bind his wretched wound up? There, 'tis stanched,
And he revives! Antonio, speak to me,
I am Philóta,—thine own, own Philóta.

Antonio, [*his mind wandering.*]

Where hast thou been, my love, this weary time?—
Am I not true?—I charge thee, heed them not!—
The girl is nothing to me;—Rousso's tongue,

His sharp false tongue first joined our names
    together;
She loves another, and *I* love — but thee; —
Draw nearer, let me whisper. I have dreamed,
Oh, *such* a dream! — the valleys flowed with blood,
And Ruin compassed all our Island round,
And every town was sacked, — and — hark ye,
    nearer! —
I saw a mother murdered by a knave,
A coward knave, because she would not yield
Her body to him; — but I saved her child,
And here he is, — a pretty, pretty boy!
Take him, Philóta. Ah, — my heart, my heart!
It pains me sorely; — 'twas a terrible dream,
But now, thank Heaven, 'tis over! Thou art pale;
What makes thee pale? Bear up, my dearest Love!
This morn we shall be wedded, and I think
We will not part again! — I had a foe,
His name is Rousso; — but we are *so* happy,
Let us forgive all foes; invite him hither, —

          PHILOTA, [*weeping.*]

He breaks my heart —

          ANTONIO.

                  How keen the wind is!
Keen, keen, and chill; it was not wont to blow

So coldly at this season; I am sick,
Yea, sick of very joy; but joy kills not; —
My lids are heavy; I would sleep, Philóta.
Wake me at early dawn; I told my mother,
That I would bring thee home, to-morrow morn.

[*He dies.*]

ALLAN HERBERT.

SCENE I.

[The hall of a country house in Westmoreland, surrounded with portraits of the M..... family. ALLAN HERBERT, and JOCELYN, an old domestic, are seen standing before the likeness of a lady, young, and wonderfully fair.]

HERBERT.

The canvas speaks!

JOCELYN.

Aye, Sir! 'tis very like;
Was she not beautiful?

HERBERT.

Was! yes, and *is;*
She had not lost one bloom when late I saw her.

JOCELYN.

Sir, she is dead!

HERBERT.

Aye! so they say, old man;

And yet I see her nightly,—in my dreams;
I tell you that her cheek is round and fair
As summer's fulness,—that her eyes are lustrous,—
And she—a perfect Presence clasped in light!
Thus will she look, on resurrection morning.

JOCELYN, [aside.]

Alas, poor gentlemen! how many loved her,
And loved her vainly! Pardon, Sir, your name?

HERBERT.

My name is Allan Herbert.

JOCELYN.

Herbert, Herbert!
Where have I heard that dainty name before?
[Musing.]
Oh, now I have it; my young mistress, Sir,
She who is dead, was wont to read a book,—
A delicate gold-edged volume, that I'm sure
Bore some such name within it; she would sit
Beneath yon grape vine trellis toward the South,
(This window, Sir, commands it,) and for hours,
Nay, days, bend o'er her favorite pages; once
She left the book behind her, and I saw
Its leaves were drenched with tears.

HERBERT.

                Where is it now?—
That book your mistress loved? let me behold it!

JOCELYN.

In sooth, Sir, I have never seen it since,
Or — if I have, [*hesitating*] it lies beyond our reach.

HERBERT.

What meanest thou?

JOCELYN.

                I mean that while she lay
Decked for her burial, whilst I stood beside her,
Looking my last upon her tranquil features,
The robe of death was fluttered by the wind, —
A low sad wailing wind, — that swept aside
The drapery for a moment, and I marked
The glimmer of the gold-edged pages placed
Right on her bosom! Master, you are pale, —
You tremble; I have rudely touched the spring
Of some deep-seated sorrow!

HERBERT.

                Yes, old man!
A sorrow most unlike to common griefs,

That pass like clouds or shadows; mine is mingled
With the dark hues of treachery and remorse,
A rayless, blank eclipse, through which I wander,
Accursed and hopeless; sometimes in a vision
Comes the sweet face of her I foully wronged,
And stabs me with a smile! —

JOCELYN.

     Did'st wrong her, Sir?
Did'st wrong my lady?

HERBERT.

     Lead me to the grave;
I know 'tis near at hand.

JOCELYN.

     The grave! what grave?
Moreover, — *if* you wronged her ——

HERBERT.

     If I wronged her!
Why dost thou taunt me with it? thou on earth
With Mercy still beside thee, — I — in Hell?

JOCELYN.

     Madman!

HERBERT.

I am *not* mad, my friend, but only wretched;
Once more, I pray thee, show me where she sleeps.

JOCELYN.

I must obey him; this way, — follow me.
                                            [*Exeunt.*]

SCENE II.

[*A forest.* — Deep in the shade a single monument appears, covered with wild-flowers and roses.]

HERBERT, [*alone.*]

'Tis fit she should be buried in this place
So fragrant and so peaceful; O, my love!
Thou hast grown dull of hearing! I may call
'Till the lone echoes shiver with thy name,
Thou wilt not heed me; dust, dust, dust indeed!
And thou — more glorious than the morning-star;
More tender than the love-light of the eve! —
They tell me thou shalt rise again, Christ's bride,
Not mine, — most beautiful, yet *changed;*
Perchance I shall not know thee, or perchance,
The human love which made thine eyes like Heaven —
My Heaven of hope and worship — shall be lost

In some diviner splendor! — all is hushed,
No smallest whisper trembles gently up
From the deep grave to soothe me; 'tis in vain
I agonize in thought. Eternal Nature!
She whom I once called "mother," wears an aspect
Callous and pitiless. I fain would solve
This terrible mystery that weighs down my soul
With nightmare fancies. Let me die in peace,
O God! and if I may not see her more
Through all the long Eternities, nor hear
Her voice of tender pardon, let me rest
Next to some stream of Lethe, and repose
In everlasting slumbers! ———

[*Enter* Jocelyn.]

Jocelyn.

Come, let us hence! the darkness creeps upon us; —
See, Sir! there's not a spark of sunset left
In all the waning West.

Herbert.

                 Well, what of that!
I live in darkness, — the light burns my spirit,
It mocks and tortures me! Begone, I say,
And leave me to the dismal shade thou fearest!

Jocelyn.

Good Sir, be counselled, — stay not in the wood;

Thine eye is troubled, and thy visage weary;—
'Tis a rash venture!

HERBERT.

           Sooth to say, I thank thee;
Thou could'st not serve long in the household blessed
By *her* most merciful presence, and not catch
Some tenderness of temper;— take my thanks!
Yet will I stay in this same dreary wood,
And watch until the night is overpast.

JOCELYN.

Thou'lt find it lonely.

HERBERT.

           Oh, I have my thoughts,
A stirring company, that never slumber.

JOCELYN.

Why, worse and worse! I've heard, such restless
    thoughts
Engender a sore sickness——

HERBERT.

               Of the mind;—
Yet is *my* case already desperate,—
Past healing, and past comfort. Go thy way,

Thou kind old man,—thou canst not shake my purpose,—
But when the last star wanes before the dawn,
Come back; my night will then be overpast,
And my watch ended; till that hour,—farewell!

SONNET.

Through dismal nights, and long laborious days,
A weary Workman at the forge of Thought,
He toils, till brain and spirit overwrought,
Sink to enforced inaction, and the maze
Of troublous dreams;—no nimble Fancy plays
Her necromantic tricks which lead to naught
But stale delusions; bitter years have taught
His heart the hollowness of casual praise;
And yet, even this poor boon's denied him now;—
Bound by Convention's hard and galling rule,
He must subdue his nature, smooth his brow,
List meekly while an ignorant Pedant speaks,
And though the hot blood boils from soul to cheeks,
Pay homage to a tyrant, and a fool!

DRAMATIC FRAGMENTS.

(FROM THE CONSPIRATOR, AN UNPUBLISHED TRAGEDY.)

SCENE.

[A garden;—ARNOLD DE MALPAS and CATHARINE discovered walking slowly towards a summer-house in the distance.]

CATHARINE.

Art thou prepared to risk all this, De Malpas?

DE MALPAS.

Ay! this, and more, if I but thought ——
[*Hesitating.*]

CATHARINE.
                                What, Arnold?

DE MALPAS.

If I but thought that when the strife was over,
The feeble Prince hurled down, the throne secured,
She, for whose love I braved the people's hate,

Malice of rulers, and the headsman's axe,
Would deign to share with me that perilous height.

CATHARINE.

She! Oh, thou hast a lady-love!

DE MALPAS.

Cruel! Wouldst thou put by my passion thus,
With a feigned jest? Catharine, I stake my all,—
Manhood's strong hopes and purpose, the heart's wealth,
And the mind's store of hard-bought lore,— my peace
Of conscience, and my soul's immortal life,
To lift *thee* to the summit of thy wish;
(Oh! I have proved thee, and I know thy thoughts,)
And yet— thou feignest ignorance!

CATHARINE.

Dear De Malpas,
Forgive me! let us both throw by the mask!
I *hate* the Queen;— even in our girlish days,
She was my rival; her mild-mannered arts
Stole suitors from me; the old Priest, our Teacher,
Though I eclipsed her ever in the school,
And shamed her dullness with keen-witted words
And quicker apprehension, shone on her

With sunny aspect, sleeked her golden hair,
Fondled and soothed and petted, whilst for *me* —
The apter scholar — he reserved harsh looks,
And harsher tones; — (Well, the old fool is dead!
In after time, *some* friend of Holy Church —
Some zealous friend — proved that his saintship taught
Schism and heresy, and so — he perished!)
But for this Queen, this Eleanor! our souls
Nursed yearly a more fixed hostility;
We sat together at the knightly jousts,
And watched the conflict with high beating hearts,
Flushed cheeks, and fluttering pulses, — *she* from fear,
I with the mounting heat of martial blood,
Thrilled with the music of the battle's roar,
The ring of mighty lances on steel helms,
Clangor of shields, and neighing of wild steeds: —
One morn MY knight was victor; — as he placed
The crown of gems and laurel on my brow,
Methought that I was born to be a queen, —
Not the brief ruler of a festal throng,
But 'stablished kingdoms, and a host of men
Bound to my sway forever!

    DE MALPAS.
      A true thought!

O, nobler Catharine! thy aspiring spirit
Fires my purpose, and gives wings to action;
Thy rival hath sped past thee in the race,—
But she shall fall midway; the blinded Monarch
Walks on the brink of an abysmal deep,
And soon shall topple over; *then*, a victor,
(Not from the conflict with half-blunted spears
In friendly tournament,) — but the tumult fierce
Of revolution, and the crash of states,
Shall set a weightier crown about thy brows,
And hail thee ruler, — *not of festal throngs,
But 'stablished kingdoms, and a host of men
Bound to thy sway forever!*

(*From the same.*)

ARNOLD DE MALPAS.

Speak, Bolton! what say these, my faithful friends,
Touching my present life?

BOLTON.

Why, Master Arnold,
I' sooth they're much divided; some assert,
That thou art moonstruck; that some morbid fancy,
Whether of love or pride, hath seized upon thee;
Others, that thou hast simply lost thy trust
In man and in thyself;— and others still,

That thou hast sunk to base, inglorious ease,
Urging the languid currents of the blood
With fiery spurs of sense; a few there are,—
Few, but most faithful,— who at dead of night
In secret conclave, with low-whispered words
And pallid faces glancing back aghast,
Speak of a monstrous wrong, which thou——

ARNOLD DE MALPAS.

[*Starting up, and seizing* BOLTON.]

Unhappy wretch! therein thou speak'st thy doom!
That prying, curious spirit is thy Fate.
        [*Stabs him suddenly.*]
Did I not warn thee of it?

BOLTON.

                  Oh! I die!
Yet my soul swells and lightens; all the future
Flashes before me like a revelation.
Arnold De Malpas! thou shalt gain thine end!
The aged king shall fall, the throne be thine!
But,— as thou goest to claim it, as thy foot
Presses the royal daïs, (mark my words!)
A bolt shall fall from Heaven, sudden, swift,
Even as thy blow on me,— thou'lt writhe i' the dust,
Down-trodden by the hostile heels of thousands,
Whilst *she*, for whom thou'st turned Conspirator,

Smiling, shall gaze from out her palace doors,
And wave her broidered scarf, and join the music
Of her low witching laughter to the sneers
Of courtly parasites; "De Malpas bore
His honors bravely,— did he not my Lords?
Now, by our Lady, 'tis a grievous fall!"
"Yet pride, thou know'st, sweet Catharine,"—
                    "Aye, aye, aye!—
"Prithee Francisco, wilt thou dance to-night?"

ARNOLD.

What, fool! wilt prate forever? hence, I say,
And entertain the devil with thy dreamings!
        [*Stabs him again.*]

(*From the Same.*)

ARNOLD.

Thou hast been to court, Bernaldi, hast thou not?

BERNALDI.

Ay! all the forenoon!

ARNOLD.

            Didst thou see the lady,—
Catharine of Savoy, whose miraculous beauty
Hath set all Spain aflame?

BERNALDI.

                      I did, my cousin,
But — I am bold to speak it — liked her not;
Her beauty is the beauty of the serpent,
Masking a poisonous spirit; — there's no depth
Of womanly nature in her gleaming eyes, —
Falsest when most they flatter; men have said
She owns the Borgia's blood; I know not that,
But, by St. Mark! she owns their temper, cousin!

DRAMATIC FRAGMENT.

We might have been! ah, yes! we might have been
Amongst the crownéd noblemen of Thought,
Who lift their species with them as they climb
To deathless empire in the realm of Gods;
But some dark power — we will not call it Fate —
We dare not call it Providence — hath seized
The helm of our strange destinies, and steered
Right onward to the breakers. All is lost!
Hope's syren song of promise faints in sighs,
And Bliss! (but SHE ne'er charmed us, save in days
Of dim-remembered childhood;) let it pass!
Our lot's the lot of millions; for on life
A blight is preying, and a mystic wrong
Hath set our heartstrings to the tune of Grief!

THE PENITENT.

Thou see'st yon woman with the grave pelisse
Lined with dark sables? Is she not devout?
Her soul is in the service, and her eyes
Are dim with weeping, — weeping for the follies
Of a misguided youth; thus saith the world,
But *I*, who *know* her ladyship, know this:
She weeps *that youth itself,* and the lost triumphs
Which followed in its train; the scores of lovers
Dead now, or married off; the rout, the joust,
The sweet flirtations, merry carnivals,
And — (oh! supremest memory of all!)
The banded serenaders 'neath the lattice,
Lifting the voice of passion in the night:
And one amongst the minstrels loved her well,
But him she laughed to scorn, his heart was riven;
She trampled on the purest pearl of love,
And cast it to the dogs; well, God is just!
She scorned *His* sacred gift, and so must walk,
Henceforth, a lonely woman on the earth!

A LIFE-HISTORY, — BRIEFLY TOLD.

I.

In the saddening light of the Autumn stars,
Half hidden behind those lattice-bars, —
I mark the flush of her ringlets bright
Gleam faintly forth on the misty night;

II.

Her face is pale, and I barely see
That her looks are bended mournfully
On what, perchance, is the image of One,
Who, dying, — left her hopes undone!

III.

Poor girl! she had given her best, her all, —
And now her heart like a funeral pall
Holds only a thought of the silent dead,
Of the grace that is lost, and the love that's fled.

TO G. C. H.

I.

I know not where thou art my Friend,
But tender thoughts arise, and wend
Their way to thee, *where'er* thou art;
No distance chills the loyal heart.

II.

If ocean breezes fan thy cheek,
Oh, may their breath be mild and meek,
And every wind that stirs the sea
Come like a mother's kiss to thee!

III.

Or if, the mighty billows past,
Thy eager feet have touched at last
That glorious realm which filled thy dreams,
While pondering by our Western streams,

IV.

May all those antique scenes be bright
As when beheld in Fancy's light,

So that thy soul may haply chance
To wander still with old Romance.

v.

Once, the delicious hope was mine
To blend a traveller's joys with thine,
From farthest frith of Northern sea,
To the fair fields of Italy:

vi.

But Fate stepped in with stern command,
And bound me to this barren land;—
What matter?—though by Fate denied,
No Power can keep me from thy side.

LINES

ON THE BUST OF A BACCHANTE, BY ALEXANDER GALT, OF VIRGINIA.

Thou Image of sweet passion crowned with hope,
  Thou glorious Personation of flushed youth,
  Lost in the fresh dawn of a mystic truth,
  Whose hidden motion hath o'erpast the scope
Of maiden wisdom — thy bewildering face
  Thrilling beyond the marble — thy glad port
  Of eager exaltation, where the sport
  Of a child's nature, chastened by the grace
Of thy maturer spirit's subtlest sense,
  Breaks into starry sparkles of still bliss —
  These hold me spelled, and breathless, and dispense
Faint languors round me, and a radiant air
  Like some serenest morning's, touched to rare
  Voluptuous beauty by Apollo's kiss.

THE REALM OF REST.

In the realm that Nature boundeth,
Are there balmy shores of peace,
Where no passion-torrent soundeth,
And no storm-wind seeks release?
Rest they 'mid the waters golden,
Of some undiscovered sea,
Where low, Halcyon airs have stolen,
Lingering round them slumbrously?

Shores begirt by purple hazes,
Varying with pale, mellowed beams,
Whose dim curtains shroud the mazes,
Wandering through a realm of dreams;
Shores, where Silence woos Devotion,
Action faints, and Echo dies,
And each peace-entranced emotion
Feeds on quiet mysteries.

If there be, Oh, guardian Master!
Genius of my life and fate,
Bear me from the world's disaster,
Through that Kingdom's shadowy gate;

Let me rest beneath its willows,
On the fragrant, flowering strand,
Lulled to sleep by murmurous billows,
Thrilled with gales of Elfin-land.

Slumber, flushed with faintest dreamings;
Deep that knows no answering deep,
Unprofaned by phantom-seemings,
Which but leave the soul to weep;
Noiseless, timeless, *half* forgetting,
Let that sleep Elysian be,
Whilst serener tides are setting,
Inward, from a roseate sea.

Soft to mine a voice is calling,
Sweet as Tropic winds at night,
Gently sighing, faintly falling
From some wondrous, mystic height,
And it gives my soul assurance,
Of the land I long to know,
Nerving to a fresh endurance,
'Neath the present weight of woe.

"There's a Realm, thy footsteps nearing,"
[Thus the voice to mine replies,]
"Where the heavy heart's despairing
Gains its rest, and stops its sighs;

THE REALM OF REST.

'Tis a realm, imperial, stately,
Refuge of dethronèd Years,
Calm as Midnight, towering greatly,
Through a moonlit mist of tears.

"Though an Empire, freedom reigneth,
Kingly brow and subject knee,
Each with what to each pertaineth,
Slumbering in equality;
'Tis a sleep, divorced from dreamings,
Deep that knows no answering deep,
Unprofaned by phantom-seemings —
Noiseless, wondrous, timeless sleep.

"On its shores are weeping willows,
Action faints, and Echo dies,
And the languid dirge of billows,
Lulls with opiate symphonies;
But beside that murmurous Ocean
All who rest, repose in sooth,
And no more the stilled emotion
Stirs to joy, or wakens ruth.

"Thou *shalt* gain these blest dominions,
Thou *shalt* find this peaceful ground,
Shaded by Oblivion's pinions,
Startled by no mortal sound;

Noiseless, timeless, ALL forgetting,
Shall thy sleep Elysian be,
Whilst eternal tides are setting
Inward from that mystic sea.

☞ Any Books in this list will be sent free of postage, on receipt of price.

BOSTON, 135 WASHINGTON STREET,
NOVEMBER, 1859.

A LIST OF BOOKS

PUBLISHED BY

TICKNOR AND FIELDS.

Sir Walter Scott.

ILLUSTRATED HOUSEHOLD EDITION OF THE WAVERLEY NOVELS. In portable size, 16mo. form. Now Complete. Price 75 cents a volume.

The paper is of fine quality; the stereotype plates are not old ones repaired, the type having been cast expressly for this edition. The Novels are illustrated with capital steel plates engraved in the best manner, after drawings and paintings by the most eminent artists, among whom are Birket Foster, Darley, Billings, Landseer, Harvey, and Faed. This Edition contains all the latest notes and corrections of the author, a Glossary and Index; and some curious additions, especially in "Guy Mannering" and the "Bride of Lammermoor;" being the fullest edition of the Novels ever published. *The notes are at the foot of the page,*—a great convenience to the reader.

Any of the following Novels sold separate.

WAVERLEY, 2 vols.
GUY MANNERING, 2 vols.
THE ANTIQUARY, 2 vols.
ROB ROY, 2 vols.
OLD MORTALITY, 2 vols.
BLACK DWARF, }
LEGEND OF MONTROSE, } 2 vols.
HEART OF MID LOTHIAN, 2 vols.
BRIDE OF LAMMERMOOR, 2 vols.
IVANHOE, 2 vols.
THE MONASTERY, 2 vols.
THE ABBOT, 2 vols.
KENILWORTH, 2 vols.
THE PIRATE, 2 vols.
THE FORTUNES OF NIGEL, 2 vols.
PEVERIL OF THE PEAK, 2 vols.
QUENTIN DURWARD, 2 vols.
ST. RONAN'S WELL, 2 vols.
REDGAUNTLET, 2 vols.
THE BETROTHED, } 2 vols.
THE HIGHLAND WIDOW, }
THE TALISMAN,
TWO DROVERS,
MY AUNT MARGARET'S MIRROR, } 2 vols.
THE TAPESTRIED CHAMBER,
THE LAIRD'S JOCK.
WOODSTOCK, 2 vols.
THE FAIR MAID OF PERTH, 2 vols.
ANNE OF GEIERSTEIN, 2 vols.
COUNT ROBERT OF PARIS, 2 vols.
THE SURGEON'S DAUGHTER, }
CASTLE DANGEROUS, } 2 vols.
INDEX AND GLOSSARY.

Thomas De Quincey.

CONFESSIONS OF AN ENGLISH OPIUM-EATER, AND SUSPIRIA DE PROFUNDIS. With Portrait. 75 cents.
BIOGRAPHICAL ESSAYS. 75 cents.
MISCELLANEOUS ESSAYS. 75 cents.
THE CÆSARS. 75 cents.
LITERARY REMINISCENCES. 2 vols. $1.50.
NARRATIVE AND MISCELLANEOUS PAPERS. 2 vols. $1.50
ESSAYS ON THE POETS, &c. 1 vol. 16mo. 75 cents.
HISTORICAL AND CRITICAL ESSAYS. 2 vols. $1.50.
AUTOBIOGRAPHIC SKETCHES. 1 vol. 75 cents.
ESSAYS ON PHILOSOPHICAL WRITERS, &c. 2 vols. 16mo. $1.50.
LETTERS TO A YOUNG MAN, and other Papers. 1 vol. 75 cents.
THEOLOGICAL ESSAYS AND OTHER PAPERS. 2 vols. $1.50.
THE NOTE BOOK. 1 vol. 75 cents.
MEMORIALS AND OTHER PAPERS. 2 vols. 16mo. $1.50.
THE AVENGER AND OTHER PAPERS. 1 vol. 75 cents.
LOGIC OF POLITICAL ECONOMY, and other Papers. 1 vol. 75 cents.

Alfred Tennyson.

POETICAL WORKS. With Portrait. 2 vols. Cloth. $2.00.
POCKET EDITION OF POEMS COMPLETE. 75 cents.
THE PRINCESS. Cloth. 50 cents.
IN MEMORIAM. Cloth. 75 cents.
MAUD, AND OTHER POEMS. Cloth. 50 cents.
IDYLS OF THE KING. A new volume. Cloth. 75 cents.

Barry Cornwall.

ENGLISH SONGS AND OTHER SMALL POEMS. $1.00.
DRAMATIC POEMS. Just published. $1.00.
ESSAYS AND TALES IN PROSE. 2 vols. $1.50.

Henry W. Longfellow.

POETICAL WORKS. In two volumes. 16mo. Boards. $2.00.
POCKET EDITION OF POETICAL WORKS. In two volumes. $1.75.
POCKET EDITION OF PROSE WORKS COMPLETE. In two volumes. $1.75.
THE SONG OF HIAWATHA. $1.00.
EVANGELINE: A TALE OF ACADIE. 75 cents.
THE GOLDEN LEGEND. A POEM. $1.00.
HYPERION. A ROMANCE. $1.00.
OUTRE-MER. A PILGRIMAGE. $1.00.
KAVANAGH. A TALE. 75 cents.
THE COURTSHIP OF MILES STANDISH. 1 vol. 16mo. 75 cents.
Illustrated editions of EVANGELINE, POEMS, HYPERION, THE GOLDEN LEGEND, and MILES STANDISH.

Charles Reade.

PEG WOFFINGTON. A NOVEL. 75 cents.
CHRISTIE JOHNSTONE. A NOVEL. 75 cents.
CLOUDS AND SUNSHINE. A NOVEL. 75 cents.
'NEVER TOO LATE TO MEND.' 2 vols. $1.50.
WHITE LIES. A NOVEL. 1 vol. $1.25.
PROPRIA QUÆ MARIBUS and THE BOX TUNNEL. 25 cts.

William Howitt.

LAND, LABOR, AND GOLD. 2 vols. $2.00.
A BOY'S ADVENTURES IN AUSTRALIA. 75 cents.

James Russell Lowell.

COMPLETE POETICAL WORKS. In Blue and Gold. 2 vols. $1.50.
POETICAL WORKS. 2 vols. 16mo. Cloth. $1.50
SIR LAUNFAL. New Edition. 25 cents.
A FABLE FOR CRITICS. New Edition. 50 cents.
THE BIGLOW PAPERS. A New Edition. 63 cents.

Nathaniel Hawthorne.

TWICE-TOLD TALES. Two volumes. $1.50.
THE SCARLET LETTER. 75 cents.
THE HOUSE OF THE SEVEN GABLES. $1.00.
THE SNOW IMAGE, AND OTHER TALES. 75 cents.
THE BLITHEDALE ROMANCE. 75 cents.
MOSSES FROM AN OLD MANSE. 2 vols. $1.50.
TRUE STORIES FROM HISTORY AND BIOGRAPHY. With four fine Engravings. 75 cents.
A WONDER-BOOK FOR GIRLS AND BOYS. With seven fine Engravings. 75 cents.
TANGLEWOOD TALES. Another "Wonder-Book." With Engravings. 88 cents.

Oliver Wendell Holmes.

POEMS. With fine Portrait. Boards. $1.00. Cloth. $1.12.
ASTRÆA. Fancy paper. 25 cents.

Charles Kingsley.

TWO YEARS AGO. A New Novel. $1.25.
AMYAS LEIGH. A Novel $1.25.
GLAUCUS; OR, THE WONDERS OF THE SHORE. 50 cts.
POETICAL WORKS. 75 cents.
THE HEROES; OR, GREEK FAIRY TALES. 75 cents.
ANDROMEDA AND OTHER POEMS. 50 cents.
SIR WALTER RALEIGH AND HIS TIME, &c. $1.25.

Coventry Patmore.

THE ANGEL IN THE HOUSE. BETROTHAL.
"   "   "   "   ESPOUSALS. 75 cts. each.

Charles Sumner.

ORATIONS AND SPEECHES. 2 vols. $2.50.
RECENT SPEECHES AND ADDRESSES. $1.25.

John G. Whittier.

Pocket Edition of Poetical Works. 2 vols. $1.50.
Old Portraits and Modern Sketches. 75 cents.
Margaret Smith's Journal. 75 cents.
Songs of Labor, and other Poems. Boards. 50 cts.
The Chapel of the Hermits. Cloth. 50 cents.
Literary Recreations, &c. Cloth. $1.00.
The Panorama, and other Poems. Cloth. 50 cents.

Alexander Smith.

A Life Drama. 1 vol. 16mo. 50 cents.
City Poems. With Portrait. 1 vol. 16mo. 63 cents.

Bayard Taylor.

Poems of Home and Travel. Cloth. 75 cents.
Poems of the Orient. Cloth. 75 cents.

Edwin P. Whipple.

Essays and Reviews. 2 vols. $2.00.
Lectures on Literature and Life. 63 cents.
Washington and the Revolution. 20 cents.

George S. Hillard.

Six Months in Italy. 1 vol. 16mo. $1.50.
Dangers and Duties of the Mercantile Profession. 25 cents.
Selections from the Writings of Walter Savage Landor. 1 vol. 16mo. 75 cents.

Robert Browning.

Poetical Works. 2 vols. $2.00.
Men and Women. 1 vol. $1.00.

Henry Giles.

LECTURES, ESSAYS, &c. 2 vols. $1.50.
DISCOURSES ON LIFE. 75 cents.
ILLUSTRATIONS OF GENIUS. Cloth. $1.00.

William Motherwell.

COMPLETE POETICAL WORKS. In Blue and Gold. 1 vol. 75 cents.
MINSTRELSY, ANC. AND MOD. 2 vols. Boards. $1.50.

Capt. Mayne Reid.

THE PLANT HUNTERS. With Plates. 75 cents.
THE DESERT HOME: OR, THE ADVENTURES OF A LOST FAMILY IN THE WILDERNESS. With fine Plates. $1.00.
THE BOY HUNTERS. With fine Plates. 75 cents.
THE YOUNG VOYAGEURS: OR, THE BOY HUNTERS IN THE NORTH. With Plates. 75 cents.
THE FOREST EXILES. With fine Plates. 75 cents.
THE BUSH BOYS. With fine Plates. 75 cents.
THE YOUNG YAGERS. With fine Plates. 75 cents.
RAN AWAY TO SEA: AN AUTOBIOGRAPHY FOR BOYS. With fine Plates. 75 cents.
THE BOY TAR: A VOYAGE IN THE DARK. A New Book. (In Press.)

Goethe.

WILHELM MEISTER. Translated by *Carlyle*. 2 vols. $2.50.
FAUST. Translated by *Hayward*. 75 cents.
FAUST. Translated by *Charles T. Brooks*. $1.00.
CORRESPONDENCE WITH A CHILD. *Bettini*. (In Press.)

Rev. Charles Lowell.

PRACTICAL SERMONS. 1 vol. 12mo. $1.25.
OCCASIONAL SERMONS. With fine Portrait. $1.25.

Rev. F. W. Robertson.

SERMONS. First Series. $1.00.
" Second " $1.00.
" Third " $1.00.
" Fourth " $1.00. (In Press.)
LECTURES AND ADDRESSES ON LITERARY AND SOCIAL TOPICS. $1.00.

R. H. Stoddard.

POEMS. Cloth. 63 cents.
ADVENTURES IN FAIRY LAND. 75 cents.
SONGS OF SUMMER. 75 cents.

George Lunt.

LYRIC POEMS, &c. Cloth. 63 cents.
JULIA. A Poem. 50 cents.
THREE ERAS OF NEW ENGLAND. $1.00.

Philip James Bailey.

THE MYSTIC, AND OTHER POEMS. 50 cents.
THE ANGEL WORLD, &c. 50 cents.
THE AGE, A SATIRE. 75 cents.

Anna Mary Howitt.

AN ART STUDENT IN MUNICH. $1.25.
A SCHOOL OF LIFE. A Story. 75 cents.

Mary Russell Mitford.

OUR VILLAGE. Illustrated. 2 vols. 16mo. $2.50.
ATHERTON, AND OTHER STORIES. 1 vol. 16mo. $1.25.

Josiah Phillips Quincy.

LYTERIA: A DRAMATIC POEM. 50 cents.
CHARICLES: A DRAMATIC POEM. 50 cents.

Grace Greenwood.

GREENWOOD LEAVES. 1st & 2d Series. $1.25 each.
POETICAL WORKS. With fine Portrait. 75 cents.
HISTORY OF MY PETS. With six fine Engravings. Scarlet cloth. 50 cents.
RECOLLECTIONS OF MY CHILDHOOD. With six fine Engravings. Scarlet cloth. 50 cents.
HAPS AND MISHAPS OF A TOUR IN EUROPE. $1.25.
MERRIE ENGLAND. A new Juvenile. 75 cents.
A FOREST TRAGEDY, AND OTHER TALES. $1.00.
STORIES AND LEGENDS. A new Juvenile. 75 cents.

Mrs. Crosland.

LYDIA: A WOMAN'S BOOK. Cloth. 75 cents.
ENGLISH TALES AND SKETCHES. Cloth. $1.00.
MEMORABLE WOMEN. Illustrated. $1.00.

Mrs. Jameson.

CHARACTERISTICS OF WOMEN. Blue and Gold. 75 cents.
LOVES OF THE POETS. " " 75 cents.
DIARY OF AN ENNUYÉE. " " 75 cents.
SKETCHES OF ART, &c. " " 75 cents.
STUDIES AND STORIES. " " 75 cents.
ITALIAN PAINTERS. " " 75 cents.

Mrs. Mowatt.

AUTOBIOGRAPHY OF AN ACTRESS. $1.25.
PLAYS. ARMAND AND FASHION. 50 cents.
MIMIC LIFE. 1 vol. $1.25.
THE TWIN ROSES. 1 vol. 75 cents.

Mrs. Howe.

PASSION FLOWERS. 75 cents.
WORDS FOR THE HOUR. 75 cents.
THE WORLD'S OWN. 50 cents.

Alice Cary.

POEMS. 1 vol. 16mo. $1.00.
CLOVERNOOK CHILDREN. With Plates. 75 cents.

Mrs. Eliza B. Lee.

MEMOIR OF THE BUCKMINSTERS. $1.25.
FLORENCE, THE PARISH ORPHAN. 50 cents.
PARTHENIA. 1 vol. 16mo. $1.00.

Samuel Smiles.

LIFE OF GEORGE STEPHENSON: ENGINEER. $1.00.

Blanchard Jerrold.

DOUGLAS JERROLD'S WIT. 75 cents.
LIFE AND LETTERS OF DOUGLAS JERROLD. $1.00.

Mrs. Judson.

ALDERBROOK. By *Fanny Forrester*. 2 vols. $1.75.
THE KATHAYAN SLAVE, AND OTHER PAPERS. 1 vol. 63 cents.
MY TWO SISTERS: A SKETCH FROM MEMORY. 50 cents.

Trelawny.

RECOLLECTIONS OF SHELLEY AND BYRON. 75 cents.

Charles Sprague.

POETICAL AND PROSE WRITINGS. With fine Portrait. Boards. 75 cents.

Mrs. Lawrence.

LIGHT ON THE DARK RIVER: OR MEMOIRS OF MRS. HAMLIN. 1 vol. 16mo. Cloth. $1.00.

G. A. Sala.
A Journey due North. $1.00.

Thomas W. Parsons.
Poems. $1.00.

John G. Saxe.
Poems. With Portrait. Boards. 63 cents. Cloth. 75 cents.
The Money King, and other Poems. 1 vol. 75 cents.

Charles T. Brooks.
German Lyrics. Translated. 1 vol. 16mo. Cloth. $1.00.

Samuel Bailey.
Essays on the Formation of Opinions and the Pursuit of Truth. 1 vol. 16mo. $1.00.

Tom Brown.
School Days at Rugby. By *An Old Boy.* 1 vol. 16mo. $1.00.
The Scouring of the White Horse, or the Long Vacation Holiday of a London Clerk. By *The Author of 'School Days at Rugby.'* 1 vol. 16mo. $1.00.

Leigh Hunt.
Poems. Blue and Gold. 2 vols. $1.50.

Gerald Massey.
Poetical Works. Blue and Gold. 75 cents.

C. W. Upham.
John C. Fremont's Life, Explorations, &c. With Illustrations. 75 cents.

W. M. Thackeray.

BALLADS. 1 vol. 16mo. 75 cents.

Charles Mackay.

POEMS. 1 vol. Cloth. $1.00.

Richard Monckton Milnes.

POEMS OF MANY YEARS. Boards. 75 cents.

George H. Boker.

PLAYS AND POEMS. 2 vols. $2.00.

Matthew Arnold.

POEMS. 75 cents.

W. Edmondstoune Aytoun.

BOTHWELL. 75 cents.

Mrs. Rosa V. Johnson.

POEMS. 1 vol. 16mo. $1.00.

Henry T. Tuckerman.

POEMS. Cloth. 75 cents.

William Mountford.

THORPE: A QUIET ENGLISH TOWN, AND HUMAN LIFE THEREIN. 16mo. $1.00.

James G. Percival.

POETICAL WORKS. 2 vols. Blue and Gold. $1.75.

John Bowring.

MATINS AND VESPERS. Blue and Gold. 75 cents.

Phœbe Cary.

POEMS AND PARODIES. 75 cents.

Paul H. Hayne.

POEMS. 1 vol. 16mo. 63 cents.
AVOLIO, A LEGEND OF THE ISLAND OF COS; AND OTHER POEMS. 1 vol. *Just ready.*

Mrs. A. C. Lowell.

SEED-GRAIN FOR THOUGHT AND DISCUSSION. 2 vols. $1.75.
EDUCATION OF GIRLS. 25 cents.

G. H. Lewes.

THE LIFE AND WORKS OF GOETHE. 2 vols. 16mo. $2.50.

Lieut. Arnold.

OAKFIELD. A Novel. $1.00.

Washington Allston.

MONALDI, A TALE. 1 vol. 16mo. 75 cents.

Professor E. T. Channing.

LECTURES ON ORATORY AND RHETORIC. 75 cents.

Dr. Walter Channing.

A PHYSICIAN'S VACATION. $1.50.

Mrs. Horace Mann.

A PHYSIOLOGICAL COOKERY BOOK. 63 cents.

Arthur P. Stanley.

LIFE AND CORRESPONDENCE OF DR. ARNOLD. 2 vols. $2.00.

Christopher Wordsworth.

WILLIAM WORDSWORTH'S BIOGRAPHY. 2 vols. $2.50.

Henry Taylor.

NOTES FROM LIFE. By the Author of "Philip Van Artevelde." 1 vol. 16mo. Cloth. 63 cents.

Hufeland.

ART OF PROLONGING LIFE. Edited by Erasmus Wilson, 1 vol. 16mo. 75 cents.

Henry Kingsley.

RECOLLECTIONS OF GEOFFRY HAMLYN. A Novel. $1.25.

Dr. John C. Warren.

THE PRESERVATION OF HEALTH, &c. 1 vol. 38 cents.

James Prior.

LIFE OF EDMUND BURKE. 2 vols. $2.00.

Joseph T. Buckingham.

PERSONAL MEMOIRS AND RECOLLECTIONS OF EDITORIAL LIFE. With Portrait. 2 vols. 16mo. $1.50.

Theophilus Parsons.

A MEMOIR OF CHIEF JUSTICE THEOPHILUS PARSONS, WITH NOTICES OF SOME OF HIS CONTEMPORARIES. By his Son. With Portrait. 1 vol. 12mo. $1.50.

Goldsmith.
THE VICAR OF WAKEFIELD. Illustrated Edition. $3.00.

C. A. Bartol.
CHURCH AND CONGREGATION. $1.00.

Horace Mann.
THOUGHTS FOR A YOUNG MAN. 25 cents.

Dr. William E. Coale.
HINTS ON HEALTH. 3d Edition. 63 cents.

Lady Shelley.
SHELLEY MEMORIALS. From Authentic Sources. 1 vol. Cloth. 75 cents.

Lord Dufferin.
A YACHT VOYAGE OF 6,000 MILES. $1.00.

Fanny Kemble.
POEMS. Enlarged Edition. $1.00.

Owen Meredith.
POETICAL WORKS. Blue and Gold. 75 cents.

Arago.
BIOGRAPHIES OF DISTINGUISHED SCIENTIFIC MEN. 16mo. 2 vols. $2.00.

William Smith.
THORNDALE, OR THE CONFLICT OF OPINIONS. $1.25.

R. H. Dana, Jr.

TO CUBA AND BACK, a Vacation Voyage, by the Author of "Two Years before the Mast." 75 cents.

John Neal.

TRUE WOMANHOOD. A Novel. 1 vol. $1.25.

SWORD AND GOWN. By the Author of "Guy Livingstone." 1 vol. 75 cents.

ALMOST A HEROINE. By the Author of "Charles Auchester," and "Counterparts." 1 vol. $1.00.

TWELVE YEARS OF A SOLDIER'S LIFE: A MEMOIR OF THE LATE MAJOR W. S. R. HODSON, B. A. Edited by his Brother, Rev. George H. Hodson. 1 vol. $1.00.

GOETHE'S CORRESPONDENCE WITH A CHILD. [Bettina.] 1 vol. *Just ready.*

RAB AND HIS FRIENDS. By John Brown, M. D. 15 cents.

THE LIFE AND TIMES OF SIR PHILIP SIDNEY. 1 vol. 16mo. $1.00.

ERNEST CARROLL, OR ARTIST LIFE IN ITALY. 1 vol. 16mo. 88 cents.

CHRISTMAS HOURS. By the Author of "The Homeward Path," &c. 1 vol. 16mo. 50 cents.

MEMORY AND HOPE. Cloth. $2.00.

THALATTA; A BOOK FOR THE SEASIDE. 75 cents.

REJECTED ADDRESSES. A new edition. Cloth. 75 cents.

WARRENIANA; A COMPANION TO REJECTED ADDRESSES. 63 cents.

ANGEL VOICES. 38 cents.

THE BOSTON BOOK. $1.25.

MEMOIR OF ROBERT WHEATON. 1 vol. $1.00.

LABOR AND LOVE: A TALE OF ENGLISH LIFE. 50 cts.

THE SOLITARY OF JUAN FERNANDEZ. By the Author of Picciola. 50 cents.

WALDEN: OR, LIFE IN THE WOODS. By Henry D. Thoreau. 1 vol. 16mo. $1.00.

VILLAGE LIFE IN EGYPT. By Bayle St. John, the Author of " Purple Tints of Paris." 2 vols. 16mo. $1.25.
WENSLEY: A STORY WITHOUT A MORAL. By Edmund Quincy. 75 cents.
PALISSY THE POTTER. By Henry Morley. 2 vols. 16mo. $1.50.
THE BARCLAYS OF BOSTON. By Mrs. H. G. Otis. 1 vol. 12mo. $1.25.
SIR ROGER DE COVERLEY. By Addison. From the "Spectator." 75 cents.
SERMONS OF CONSOLATION. By F. W. P. Greenwood. $1.00.
SPAIN, HER INSTITUTIONS, POLITICS, AND PUBLIC MEN. By S. T. Wallis. $1.00.
POEMS. By Henry Alford. $1.25.

In Blue and Gold.

LONGFELLOW'S POETICAL WORKS. 2 vols. $1.75.
    do.   PROSE WORKS. 2 vols. $1.75.
TENNYSON'S POETICAL WORKS. 1 vol. 75 cents.
WHITTIER'S POETICAL WORKS. 2 vols. $1.50.
LEIGH HUNT'S POETICAL WORKS. 2 vols. $1.50.
GERALD MASSEY'S POETICAL WORKS. 1 vol. 75 cents.
MRS. JAMESON'S CHARACTERISTICS OF WOMEN. 75 cts.
    do.   DIARY OF AN ENNUYÉE. 1 vol. 75 cts.
    do.   LOVES OF THE POETS. 1 vol. 75 cts.
    do.   SKETCHES OF ART, &c. 1 vol. 75 cts.
    do.   STUDIES AND STORIES. 1 vol. 75 cts.
    do.   ITALIAN PAINTERS. 1 vol. 75 cents.
OWEN MEREDITH'S POEMS. 1 vol. 75 cents.
BOWRING'S MATINS AND VESPERS. 1 vol. 75 cents.
LOWELL'S (J. RUSSELL) POETICAL WORKS. 2 vols. $1.50
PERCIVAL'S POETICAL WORKS. 2 vols. $1.75.
MOTHERWELL'S POEMS. 1 vol. 75 cents.

www.ingramcontent.com/pod-product-compliance
Lightning Source LLC
Chambersburg PA
CBHW031949230426
43672CB00010B/2104